THE DISCOVERER OF OXYGEN

Joseph Priestley

BORN: March 13, 1733

DIED: February 6, 1804

Joseph Priestley's early scientific experiments were in the field of electricity. Later he became interested in gases, isolating and describing the properties of nitric oxide, ammonia, sulfur dioxide, hydrogen chloride, nitrogen, carbon dioxide. His greatest single achievement was the discovery of oxygen, to which Antoine Lavoisier also laid claim but which he was forced to rescind. Today every chemistry student is taught the results of Priestley's experiments—and the highest honor one can achieve in the chemical world is the Joseph Priestley medal given by The American Chemical Society "For Distinguished Service to Chemistry."

Books by William D. Crane

CANCER, COCAINE AND COURAGE
  The Story of Dr. William Halsted
  (with Arthur J. Beckhard)

THE DISCOVERER OF OXYGEN
  Joseph Priestley

THE MAN WHO TRANSFORMED THE WORLD
  James Watt

THE DISCOVERER OF OXYGEN

Joseph Priestley

by WILLIAM D. CRANE

Julian Messner, Inc.

New York

Published by Julian Messner, Inc.
8 West 40th Street, New York 18

Published simultaneously in Canada
by The Copp Clark Publishing Co. Limited

Second Printing, 1963

Printed in the United States of America

Library of Congress Catalog Card No. 62-15417

To Peg

Acknowledgment

The author wishes to thank Professor Arthur Sweeney Jr., head of the chemistry department of Hunter College, and the librarians of the Chemists' Club library for their generous cooperation.

Author's Note

Joseph Priestley was primarily a student and preacher of the Gospel. He spoke of it often as "my beloved theology." His interests, though, were almost endless, and he succeeded in making a magnificent synthesis of them all, using religion as a catalyst.

There are two particular awards given in honor of Priestley which truly sum up his contribution to this world. The American Chemical Society gives the Priestley medal "For Distinguished Service to Chemistry," and Dickinson College awards annually a Wedgwood portrait of Priestley and one thousand dollars for "Research, discovery or production benefiting mankind."

THE DISCOVERER OF OXYGEN

Joseph Priestley

Chapter One

The little town of Northumberland, Pennsylvania, was astir early on Tuesday, July 31, 1874. This might have been because it was such a clear, beautiful, cloudless day, but there was definitely something else in the air. Although several hundred strangers were in town, somehow they didn't seem like strangers. There was much going in and out of houses, many greetings and conversations in the streets and shops, and a general air of mutual understanding.

By nine o'clock the meeting room in the public school was crowded to overflowing. There were important-looking men sitting on a raised platform with important-looking papers in front of them, and other important-looking men sitting in the audience. They had come long distances and with great difficulty for this occasion, from the states of Indiana, New York, Michigan, Massachusetts, Virginia, Connecticut and Ohio, and even from Canada and England.

There were among them many men of national and international importance. There was Charles W. Mollet, professor of chemistry at the University of Virginia, one of the outstanding exponents of chemical research in America. He had been in charge of the manufacture of munitions for the Confederacy during the late Civil War, and was also famous for having determined the atomic weight of gold. Sitting near him on the platform was Thomas Sterry Hunt, founder of Laval University, professor of geology at the Canadian University of McGill, a member of the Royal Society of London and the National Academy of Science. In the audience were J. Lawrence Smith, one of the first American chemists recognized and signally honored outside of America, having been decorated by the Turkish government and awarded the Legion of Honor by France, and Frank W. Clarke, the dean of American industrial chemists and professor of chemistry at the College of Physicians and Surgeons in New York City.

There were many others of similar fame, all connected in some way with the science of chemistry. They had all come to the little Pennsylvania town from their distant homes willingly and enthusiastically. Others who had been prevented from coming had written letters expressing their deep regret at not being able to attend.

An inquisitive stranger might well have asked what all the commotion was about and what great person or event had brought to the quiet little town on the banks of the Susquehanna such a distinguished group of men, together with their wives and friends. He would have had his answer as Colonel Charles F. Chandler, a prominent citizen of Northumberland, rose to make the opening speech. He welcomed those present, commented on the beauty of the day and the distinguished nature of the audience, and reminded them that they were assembled to commemorate a great discovery and to do honor to an illustrious name, that of the good and great man who laid the cornerstone of chemical science—Joseph Priestley.

The discovery and isolation of oxygen gas, the speaker pointed out, was probably the most important single contribution to the world, although so many extraordinary advances had been made in science since, that people were apt to take as a matter of course the existence of this vital oxygen air. One could forget so easily that this colorless, tasteless, odorless gas is the most abundant of the elements, present in all living things—a veritable elixir of life. It had been and would continue to be the cause of saving thousands of lives threatened by serious respiratory diseases. He informed his listeners that the next day, August 1, had been officially named "Oxygen Day," but that today was to be devoted to oxygen's discoverer, the same man who gave the world carbon dioxide, ammonia, hydrogen chloride, muriatic acid, hydrogen sulfide, nitric oxide, nitrous oxide, sulfur dioxide and carbon monoxide.

Colonel Chandler's speech was followed by others. It was proposed that a national chemical society should be founded and that, in honor of Joseph Priestley, it should date its origin from this day. There was much talk, there was lunch, there was a visit to Priestley's laboratory, there was tea. Then, in the late afternoon, the assembled chemists and their companions moved to a pleasant hilltop graveyard outside the town. It was a pretty spot, tree shaded and overlooking the Susquehanna River, sparkling in the afternoon sun as it flowed past the towns of Northumberland and Sunbury.

There was a quiet dignity about the place which transferred itself to the men and women who entered it, and like silent ghosts they formed a semicircle around a simple marble headstone. Mr. Henry Coppee, president of Lehigh University, stopped beside the grave.

"The man who is buried here," he said, "was a chemist, a theologian, a political economist, a civilian, a physicist, a student of history and a teacher of men. But above all these things he was an ardent champion of truth and right. Seventy years ago he died regretting that he must abandon the pursuit of truth on earth.

"We approach this tomb, not in sorrow but in triumph; because he was a great scientist; because he brought his labor and his fame from intolerant England to a welcoming America; because he was a man of large and varied learning; because he was a righteous man, honest, true, just and pure.

"This is an unusual celebration. This peaceful field, an acre of God at this most charming hour, these surrounding hills, this gleaming river which lend breadth and beauty to the landscape; this distinguished assemblage standing reverently but not mournfully around a grave. These do not tell us of death, but of life, not of oblivion but of immortality."

The speaker stopped. For a moment there was no sound from the group, as their eyes raised to the headstone in front of them. The setting sun brought out the shadows of the carved inscription for all to read.

TO
THE MEMORY OF THE
REVEREND DR. JOSEPH PRIESTLEY
WHO DEPARTED THIS LIFE
ON THE 6 OF FEBRUARY, 1804

RETURN UNTO THY REST, O, MY SOUL
FOR THE LORD HATH DEALT BOUNTIFULLY WITH THEE.
I WILL LAY ME DOWN IN PEACE AND SLEEP TILL
I AWAKE IN THE MORNING OF THE RESURRECTION.

The quiet twilight crept over the field as the crowd moved silently away.

Chapter Two

Time in reality moves forward, but in memory it has a way of turning back and bringing past events into sharp focus. In 1744, one hundred and thirty years before this meeting on the banks of the Susquehanna, the man who was being so signally honored was only a scared little boy sitting in a chair by a large desk.

The chair squeaked at the least movement, although Joseph Priestley, aged eleven, did his best to stay quite motionless. This was not easy as he had sometimes to shoo away a fly or scratch his ear, but it was very important. Behind the large desk in front of him sat two people whom he had no wish to offend. One was Mr. Hogue, headmaster of the Batley School in the north of England, and the other was Joseph's aunt, Sarah Keighley. They were talking about him, which made his position even more difficult. Joseph heard most of the conversation, but occasionally the voices were lowered and he would catch a glance in his direction or the raising of an eyebrow. These moments made him very uncomfortable and the conversation seemed to go on for hours. Finally his aunt rose, patted his hand, smiled at Mr. Hogue and left him alone with the headmaster.

Mr. Hogue eyed the boy in front of him. There was nothing particularly unusual about him except that he seemed fragile and stuttered occasionally. He studied the

14

card in his hand on which he had taken careful notes during his talk with Mrs. Keighley. Joseph had been born, he noted, March 13, 1733, the son of a weaver of cloth in Fieldhead near Leeds. His mother had died when he was seven, and he was being cared for by his aunt. He was the eldest of a family of two girls and four boys, and was destined for the ministry. This last item was not surprising to Mr. Hogue as the Priestley family was deeply religious. They did not go along with the religion established in the sixteenth century by Henry VIII and known as the Church of England. Instead they worshiped God most devoutly in their own way, which undoubtedly pleased God more than it did George II.

These were the obvious facts about young Priestley, but during the moments when his aunt had whispered certain confidences to Mr. Hogue, he had learned things that interested him far more. Joseph, she had said, was a curious boy, forever reading books much too complicated for his age and not playing much with other children. He would wander off in the fields and woods, and lie for hours looking up at the sky or watching the fish in a brook. When he came home he asked all sorts of questions about birds flying in the air or fish breathing in water or anything else that puzzled him. She couldn't answer them, she said, adding that she hoped Mr. Hogue would have better luck.

Although not at all sure that he would, Mr. Hogue was not a man to give up without a real try. He smiled at the boy in front of him and plunged in.

"Your aunt tells me that you like to ask questions," he said as a starter.

"Y-yes, sir—I g-guess I do," Joseph answered.

"About what, for instance?" Mr. Hogue continued.

Since Joseph's curiosity covered almost everything he saw or heard about, he didn't see how he could be definite, so he answered, "Oh—t-things."

"I see," Mr. Hogue said noncommittally, and he leaned back in his chair. "Suppose you try me out on one of the—things."

Joseph was not too sure that Mr. Hogue was serious, and he looked rather questioningly at him.

"Go on," Mr. Hogue said encouragingly.

Joseph took a deep breath. "Well," he said, "I p-put some water in a pail right up to the t-top, and the middle of it was higher than the edge, but it didn't run over. I asked my uncle and aunt about it, and even Mr. Woburn, and they told me I was wrong and that it wasn't so. Then I put some spiders in a bottle, and they died. Mr. Woburn wouldn't explain that either, and then I—"

Mr. Hogue interrupted. "Who is this Mr. Woburn?" he asked.

"He's the h-head of our ch-church at Fieldhead."

"I see," Mr. Hogue said again. "We'll talk about him later. Suppose you and I try one thing at a time. You'll find a pail in the broom closet down the hall. Bring it here and we'll fill it with water."

Joseph was delighted. This was the first time anyone had shown any interest in his questions. Soon Mr. Hogue and he were adding water from a cup to the already full pail. Mr. Hogue bent down and squinted along the surface of the water. The center was definitely higher than the edge. Mr. Hogue scratched his head. "You're certainly right, Joseph, but I'm afraid I can't explain it."

It was most natural that Mr. Hogue couldn't explain it because it would be about forty years before the principle of what was to be called "capillary attraction" was discovered. The great thing to Joseph was that Mr. Hogue had listened to him. He took an instant liking to his new headmaster.

As the weeks went by, Mr. Hogue, being a clergyman, naturally talked to Joseph about religion. "So you're going to be a minister," he said one day.

"Oh, yes, sir," Joseph replied enthusiastically.

Mr. Hogue hadn't expected quite so much enthusiasm from an eleven-year-old. The boys he was used to generally wanted to be soldiers or sailors or stagecoach drivers. He raised his eyebrows slightly.

"What sort of minister do you want to be?" he asked, thinking to bring the young enthusiast down to earth with a more difficult question.

"A Dissenting minister, of course," was Joseph's prompt reply, and Mr. Hogue realized that here was a most unusual boy. His first reaction was a long-drawn-out "Oh—h."

"What is your idea of a Dissenting minister, Joseph?" he asked finally.

There was not the immediate reply that Mr. Hogue had expected. Joseph fidgeted slightly. "That's what Mr. Woburn calls it," he said hesitatingly. Here was Mr. Woburn again, and Mr. Hogue felt he had found a weak spot.

"And Mr. Woburn never explained it," he went on, "so you don't really know what it means"

"N-no, sir—n-not really. W-what does it mean?"

This was a definitely hard question to answer to an eleven-year-old boy, and Mr. Hogue thought awhile.

"A minister serves God," he said finally. "Isn't that right, Joseph?"

"Yes, sir," Joseph answered with his earlier enthusiasm.

"Well," Mr. Hogue went on, "it so happens that our king, George II, considers himself the head of the Church, and has decreed that all ministers shall serve God the way he says. Any minister who doesn't agree with him and his way of worshiping is a Dissenter. I happen to be one myself. They go by all sorts of names—Calvinist, Unitarian, Presbyterian and so forth—but you needn't bother about that. Does that make it clear?"

Joseph nodded. His opinion of Mr. Hogue rose, and he pursued his advantage.

"The Reverend Woburn," he said, "is forever talking about religious things with long names, but he never really tells me what they mean."

After a pause, Mr. Hogue said thoughtfully, "I think you're afraid of this Mr. Woburn. You mustn't be. In matters of religion especially you must stand up to anyone, even a Mr. Woburn, and insist on an answer. If you don't like the answer, say so. That's what we Dissenters are for. What are some of these things he talks about?"

There were so many that Joseph hesitated. "Well," he said finally, "he keeps talking about original sin. Does that mean that everyone is bad?" Mr. Hogue thought this one over. There was a distinct danger that he was getting in a little deep. He didn't blame an eleven-year-old boy for being puzzled.

"You know, Joseph," he answered finally, "I used to worry about that before you were born. John Bunyan had just died, and everyone was reading his *Pilgrim's Progress*. Have you read it, Joseph?"

"Y-yes," Joseph answered.

"Well, you must remember, then, that Bunyan said that original sin was like a coat of dust in a man's house, and he couldn't really straighten things out until he had swept it all away."

"Oh," Joseph said rather dubiously. Then after a pause, "Did that help you to stop worrying?"

"In a way, yes, Joseph. I looked around at everything— the trees, the flowers, the birds, the sun, the stars by night, the very air we breathe—and I didn't see much sign of dust. It occurred to me that people were thinking too much of the dust and not enough of the wonderful things God has created for us."

For Joseph this was a new way of looking at the problem. It put the mysterious questions that entered into religious talk on one side and all the beauties of nature on the other—like finding two separate worlds held together by the word of God. It delighted him.

"What did you do then?" he asked Mr. Hogue.

"I had some books in my library that I had never read, written about the time you were born. They were written by a Dutchman named Gravesande, and they were all about air and the stars and light. I read both volumes and I have never worried since."

"Can I read them?" Joseph asked eagerly. Mr. Hogue laughed. "Well, laddie," he replied, "you've been here only a few weeks, but give you a year and I wouldn't be surprised."

Joseph frowned. "But you said they were in your library," he said with his usual persistency.

"Aye, Joseph, they are, but the Dutchman wrote them in Latin, and I doubt that three weeks of that tongue would fit you to read them."

Joseph's face fell. He remembered all the books on his aunt Sarah's shelves that he couldn't read because they were written in strange tongues, and he vowed he would learn as many of these languages as possible. The first one was Latin. It was hard and not very interesting, but he was so persistent that he surprised not only himself but Mr. Hogue. By the end of the first year he was able to read Latin, slowly to be sure, but with real understanding.

One day when Joseph was thirteen, Mr. Hogue took him to his study and, seating him at his desk, took down two large volumes and put them in front of Joseph.

"I think you can make sense of these now, lad. Look them over."

Almost trembling with eagerness, Joseph opened the first of the heavy books. He read the title, *Physica Elementa Mathmatica* by Wilhelm Jakobs Gravesande. He turned to the table of contents. Many of the chapter headings contained words still too difficult for him, and he had to appeal to Mr. Hogue. There were others that he read easily: "Of the Motion of Fluids," "Of Air and Other

Elastic Fluids," "Of Fire." He had never thought of air as a fluid. Water and milk were the only fluids he had heard about, and he decided to begin with this chapter.

He learned that ordinary fluids such as milk and water could stay in a glass or bottle, and so were different from air which flowed out of everything into which it was put. In fact it flowed everywhere, around Joseph, around the school, around the whole world. All this air, he learned, was called the atmosphere.

On the second page there was an experiment. Mr. Hogue let him use two glass tubes, three feet long, that he kept away from most of the boys for fear they would be broken, and a bowl filled with mercury.

"These are hard to get, Joseph," he explained, "and very costly. I got them when I first read this book. I'll show you how they work."

Mr. Hogue took a tube and stopped up one end. Then he filled the tube with mercury and quickly put the open end into the mercury-filled bowl. Some of the mercury flowed out of the tube, but quite a column remained.

"You see, Joseph," Mr. Hogue went on, "the air is heavy though perhaps you wouldn't think it, and it presses on the mercury in the bowl, keeping the column of mercury standing in the bowl. If there were no weight the mercury would simply run out and overflow the bowl."

Joseph was fascinated. "Does it always stay at that height?" he asked.

"Good question, Joseph." Mr. Hogue enjoyed having his pupils ask questions, and he was happy to find someone who was interested in natural things. "Look here," he said, taking another tube filled with mercury and stopped at one end like the first one. "I'm going to put this tube in the mercury, but not straight up this time. I'll put it at an angle." Joseph watched carefully. "Measure the height," Mr. Hogue went on, "from the surface of the mercury in the bowl to the top of the column in each tube." Joseph measured it. "Don't tell me the height of each," Mr. Hogue said as Joseph started to speak. "Let me tell you—and then see if I'm right." He pretended to think very hard. "I would say," he said finally, "twenty nine inches in both cases."

Joseph grinned. "How did you know? he asked.

"It's always the same," Mr. Hogue answered. "A man named Evangelista Torricelli first made this experiment in 1643 and it has never changed since. That's how we can tell about changes in the weather. If it is to be quite normal the mercury stays at about that height. If the air is full of moisture it becomes less dense than dry air and presses down less on the mercury in the bowl; then the mercury in the tube naturally drops, and we can expect stormy weather. Now go ahead and read more. That is your first lesson about air."

Joesph read on and on. It was a new world opening to him, and he was fascinated. He finished the chapter on air. He learned about the air pump invented in 1652 by Otto Von Guericke, and the vacuum it created when used to pump air out of a container. He learned how sound went through the air and how fast it traveled. There were about a thousand pages, and it was slow work, but as he learned about light and color and the stars, his enthusiasm increased, and by the end of the year he had finished the first volume. The second went faster, and by the time he was fifteen he had thoroughly mastered both.

On his fifteenth birthday, his aunt told him that in order to become a minister, he must first be accepted into the Calvinist Chapel. She had arranged, she said, to have him examined as to his beliefs by Amos Woburn, the chief elder of the church. Joseph felt strongly that he would not like to be examined by Mr. Woburn. He wanted to become a minister, not only because of the memory of his mother who had been so devout, or to please his aunt who had done so much for him, but because he had convinced himself that God and a religious life were identical with all the beautiful and mysterious things in the world that he saw everywhere and had been reading about at school. Mr. Woburn represented something in religion that he didn't like, but he remembered the words of Mr. Hogue about standing up to people especially in matters of religion. Perhaps this was a God-given opportunity. He would see.

His aunt had arranged a meeting in Reverend Woburn's study. The sun was shining outside, but there was no warmth in the stern old man's sanctum. What rays did get into the room were so filtered out by the dust in the windows that they were pale and anemic. The atmosphere was heavy and smelled of a strange mixture of shoe leather and old clothes. From his comfortable chair behind the desk, the Reverend Woburn contemplated Joseph who was sitting on a hard chair in the middle of the room. Mr. Woburn blew his nose violently and cleared his throat.

The conversation was largely one-sided. In fact it could hardly be called conversation at all. Joseph's contributions were an occasional "Yes" or "I don't know." Mr. Woburn was quite evidently enjoying himself. He was laying down the law without opposition which always pleased him. Then suddenly the bomb fell. He had just informed Joseph that of course all people were born sinful and that this sin had to be wiped out before they could enter Heaven. He paused, expecting a complacent nod. Joseph didn't nod. He had been thinking very hard about what Mr. Hogue had said. He remembered the air that he breathed, the wind that cooled his face on a hot day, the birds that sang to him in the early morning from their nest above his window. Here was the opportunity he had been waiting for.

"N-no, sir, I can't believe that." Then, losing any hesitation, he stood up and walked to the front of the desk. He spoke challengingly without a stammer. "I cannot believe that a God who has created all the wonders of this world could be so wrathful as to let little babies be born with sin. If I must believe that, I cannot join your chapel."

A deep red came into the Reverend Woburn's face, and his hands clenched across his fat belly. "The Devil has been talking to you, Joseph. We will try to help you, and perhaps later the chapel can open its doors to you."

Joseph was quite sure that Mr. Hogue was not the Devil,

24

and he was equally sure that even if the doors of the Independent Chapel were quite off their hinges, he would not want to enter. He turned abruptly and walked out of the room, determined to face his two worlds alone, if necessary, but certainly not with the benefit of the Reverend Amos Woburn.

Chapter Three

It was only about a mile from Amos Woburn's house near the Independent Chapel, to Joseph's house, but it took him a long time. He walked slowly. He had a lot to think about. His defiance of the chief elder of the Calvinist Chapel was not just a matter of words. It went far deeper than that. It involved his aunt Sarah, a most pious Calvinist, and all his friends and neighbors. It might make him an outcast, but when he had risen from his chair and walked up to the Reverend Woburn's desk he had made a decision, and now walking along with only his thoughts, he realized that his decision was irrevocable whatever the consequences. He pictured to himself Paul on the road to Damascus hearing God's voice, and he felt convinced that in some mysterious way God had spoken to him also.

He knew that at home Aunt Sarah would be waiting to hear his account of the examination. Being tea time, there would be a visitor or two, probably Dissenting ministers whom it was his aunt's habit to invite. They would all be prepared to greet him and welcome him into the church with prayer and thanksgiving. How could he explain what had happened when he wasn't even sure himself? He knew that what he wanted was truth, and the long words and complicated ideas in the Calvinist doctrine made it impossible to discover it. Most of the ideas he simply could not believe, and he found more truth in the world of nature around him. As between Mr. Hogue and the Reverend Woburn, he preferred Mr. Hogue.

As he reached his house he heard voices, and recognized that of Mr. Kirkby who was to teach him Hebrew. The other man's voice was new to him. His heart beating fast, he opened the door. His aunt rose and came toward him. "Joseph, this is Mr. Haggerstone, and, of course, you know Mr. Kirkby. We've been talking about you and—"

Joseph nodded to the ministers, then whispered to his aunt. "I-I don't feel very well, Aunt Sarah. P-please—I c-can't talk now." He walked across the room and up the narrow stairs, leaving his aunt and her guests in silent bewilderment.

For three weeks Joseph did not leave his bed. He had developed a fever, and the local doctor suspected consumption. Meanwhile his rejection by the Independent Chapel became common knowledge, and many of the most ardent Calvinists put his sickness down to a visitation of God's wrath. His aunt was disappointed, but being a woman of a charitably broad outlook she told Joseph she was sorry, and said no more about it.

His illness gave Joseph a chance to do some quiet thinking. He knew positively that he wanted to be a Christian minister, but he couldn't get out of his mind the two heavy volumes he had read at the Batley School—all about air and light and stars, and he decided that it was perfectly possible, in fact appropriate, for a minister to learn all about the things God had created. It should, indeed, make him a better preacher.

A difficulty arose with his aunt Sarah. Without consulting him she arranged for his uncle Timothy, who had a business house in Europe, to employ Joseph in his office. Her argument was that Joseph was not physically suited to the arduous work of the ministry. "Besides, can you imagine a stuttering preacher?" she asked Mr. Haggerstone.

"God chooses his ministers, Mrs. Keighley," he answered after a moment's thought, "from among those who believe. I have worked with Joseph for almost three years, and I firmly believe it is God's will that he should be a Christian minister. As for his stammering—perhaps that can be cured."

When Joseph added his pleas, his aunt relented, and at the age of nineteen he entered Daventry Academy on the northern border of Northumberland for a three-year course to prepare him for the ministry.

The routine at the Academy was severe. The day began at six in the morning with readings and prayers for two hours before breakfast, lectures until early afternoon, more lectures and prayers in the evening, supper at nine and bed at ten-thirty. Joseph did not mind the schedule since he liked to be busy, but at first he had misgivings as to how he would be received because of his radical beliefs. He had, after all, been refused communion with a Calvinist Chapel. This in itself he feared would be held against him. His objections, though, went deeper than a dislike of Amos Woburn's pomposity and the confusing ideas of religious language. He wanted the whole idea of God and religion not only simplified but brought into closer relation with all the things he saw and enjoyed in the world of reality around him.

He hadn't been at Daventry more than a few weeks before he discovered that Dr. Ashworth, the head, and the other teachers professed to welcome any kind of free inquiry. At least they did until they admitted young Joseph Priestley.

Mr. Haggerstone's tutoring had advanced him in mathematics beyond the average first-year man in Daventry; he had read more deeply in scriptural history than the other students through his proficiency in Greek and Latin; he had listened by the hour to the disputes between visiting ministers at his aunt's house, and had formed very definite ideas which he was eager to discuss with any willing listener.

Dr. Ashworth listened and was suitably impressed up to a point. To him, free inquiry was an excellent thing if reserved for the privacy of the Daventry walls. Occasionally, however, outside church leaders would visit the Academy, and at such times expressions of individual opinions were slightly modified, or they had been until one day when a reverend gentleman, who happened to be a very strict Calvinist, was lecturing on the Trinity. He was earnest and sincere, his voice most persuasive, and he held his audience in rapt attention, especially Dr. Ashworth. Joseph listened too, but more critically. Soon his feelings got the better of him. All his passion for the truth flooded his mind. Daventry rules or no Daventry rules, he rose to his feet, politely interrupted the speaker, then poured forth such a stream of objections to the visitor's thoughts and words that the meeting ended in utter confusion.

Dr. Ashworth had a private but not very successful talk with Joseph. He was older, he was the head of a famous Dissenting academy, and he considered himself quite knowledgeable in matters of theology. Everything was in his favor except the young first-year student who stood before him. Joseph Priestley at the age of twenty, Dr. Ashworth learned to his amazement, had read all the works of the seventeenth century philosophers, was in the habit of reading ten folio pages of Greek every morning before breakfast, and in his spare time was writing a book with the formidable title of *Institutes of Natural and Revealed Religion*.

Learning all this, Dr. Ashworth did the only thing possible under the circumstances—he cautioned Joseph against any further expressions of opinion in public, then threw up his hands in despair. A year later, when he was asked to supply an assistant to the minister of a small congregation at a town in Suffolk, he unhesitatingly recommended Joseph Priestley.

Chapter Four

Needham Market in Suffolk, a town of no particular importance, was halfway between Ipswich and Norwich on the Waveley River. Its spiritual life centered in one church and was strictly Presbyterian, guided by the Reverend Aylmer Meadows, a somewhat superannuated clergyman of considerable means. The congregation of about one hundred souls was contented with its lot, and had dozed happily through many years of sermonizing under Mr. Meadows. They would have desired no change had not relentless age crept up on their preacher. Application was made to Daventry for an assistant, with the result that Joseph Priestley entered the hitherto undisturbed environs of Needham Market.

Joseph had no thought of being anything but useful in his new post. He was at last a Christian minister, and he filled the days of the difficult and dangerous trip from Northumberland to Suffolk in making plans for promoting religion in Needham Market. His salary, he was informed, would be thirty pounds a year, twenty of which would go for board and lodging. Since he had no financial help from his aunt Sarah, this was cutting things pretty close, but Joseph had developed a strong conviction that God orders all things for the best, and he accepted the salary without question. He was welcomed at tea by several ladies of the congregation, and entered spiritedly on his duties.

The first six months were fairly promising in spite of his stammering, which was a slight handicap in his preaching. At Mr. Meadows suggestion Joseph spent a very large part of his income on treatment by a supposed expert in London who turned out to be a quack, and no visible result came from the experiment. This failure, combined with the fact that Joseph began to find the approach to religion in Needham Market most uninspiring, brought out in him what Amos Woburn had referred to as "the Devil." He decided to stir things up a bit. While at Daventry, he had written two volumes on *Natural and Revealed Religion*, and he decided to preach a series of sermons, one on each chapter of the book. It was all very well for him to discuss God's goodness, His mercy and kindness, generalities that the Needham congregation accepted, but in his book Joseph had touched quite firmly on the unity of God, and various other highly controversial subjects distinctly objectionable to his Presbyterian congregation. He preached his first sermon. The sleepers were awakened and the ardent Trinitarians rose in a body and walked home. They spoke to Mr. Meadows who spoke to Joseph.

"You can't do this, Mr. Priestley," he objected. "You will have no congregation left."

At thirty pounds a year Joseph felt he had *some* rights, and he intended to assert them. "If I have but one left who wants to hear the truth," he replied, "I shall be content."

"What is the truth?" the Reverend Meadows asked.

Since no one had ever answered this question from the time Pontius Pilate first asked it, Joseph was not going to be drawn into any useless argument.

"I preach the truth as I see it, Mr. Meadows," he said quietly, "and I always intend to."

"You understand, I suppose," Mr. Meadows threatened, "that you will never be asked to preach from any neighboring pulpits?"

"Quite," Joseph replied. "George Whitefield, the great Methodist, preached in the fields, and Christ preached in the market place and, if necessary, I can."

This sort of attitude, while laudable, did not increase his popularity, and when he offered to teach mathematics and the classics to make a little more money, he had no applicants. He did gather a few people for twelve lectures on a new globe of the earth that had just been perfected, but the cost of the globes ate up any possible profit. Joseph put up with all this for three years, but finally feeling himself to be in a "low, despised situation," he looked around for another position.

As luck would have it, a Quaker friend of his had some connections in a town in Cheshire, known as Nantwich, where the small group of Nonconformists needed a minister. Feeling that any change would be for the better, Joseph accepted an invitation from them without question. He made the trip by sea because it was less expensive, though longer, and at the age of twenty-five found himself settled in a room over a grocery store run by a Mr. Eddowes.

His break with the Calvinists, his outspokenness at Daventry and his unpopularity at Needham had only served to increase his confidence in his point of view. He was stirred up and ready to do battle for his ideas with his

33

new Nantwich congregation. If they also walked out on him, he would simply go somewhere else and spread the gospel of natural, uncomplicated religion. "Simplicity is the seal of Truth" some great man had once said, and Joseph had taken the words for his motto. He determined to lose no time and started with his first sermon.

Rising before his new congregation, he made as much as possible out of his five feet ten inches. He took as his text the seventh chapter of St. John, and the third verse, "My Father is 'the only true God.'" He stammered, but he spoke in a loud voice that carried authority. He held forth fearlessly for the unity of God. He felt as he had when he had faced Mr. Amos Woburn nine years before. He wanted his congregation to know where he stood. Let them walk out on him. Let them punish him in any way they might see fit. He was prepared for it even as the ancient martyrs had been. He reached the end of his sermon and waited. Being prepared for anything he was not in the least prepared for nothing. There was the polite stir of polite relief. Nothing more. After the service the congregation dispersed with the usual words of greeting and well-wishing, and Joseph walked home to his room over Mr. Eddowes' store. He had expected a storm and had found a calm. It was very strange. Perhaps, he thought, he was arguing too much with people who didn't really care anyway. Perhaps he was falling into the error of which Mr. Hogue at the Batley School had spoken. Perhaps he was thinking too much of the dust and not enough of the wonders of God's world.

Then two quite unrelated things happened that served

to turn his mind definitely into other fields. The first had to do with a telescope. It was given to him by a Church of England minister in a neighboring town, the Reverend Allyn Alexander, whom he met quite casually on one of his frequent walks through the countryside. While not departing from their own particular doctrines, they had agreed on the fundamental right of men to follow the truth as they might see it. Joseph had spoken of his interest in natural things, and had quoted from Gravesande on the motion of the stars, or heavenly bodies, as Mr. Alexander preferred to call them. Shortly thereafter, the Church of England minister was transferred, and he left his small telescope with his friend with the admonition to "keep looking for more of God's wonders." Joseph did just this. He set the telescope on a stand on the roof of Mr. Eddowes' store, and every night investigated the movements of the stars by carefully plotting their positions on the field of the lens. This led quite naturally to the second unrelated incident.

Besides being the local grocer and a stout member of the Nonconformist congregation, Mr. Eddowes was a flute player, and a very good one. One beautiful, clear night, Joseph was crouching by his telescope gazing at the galaxies, when the sound of soft music floated out of an open window and drifted up toward the stars. The air was one of Whitefield's famous hymns, and although the instrument was a flute and not a harp, there seemed a certain divine connection between it and the heavenly bodies. Joseph was intrigued.

The next day he asked Mr. Eddowes if he could teach him to play the flute, offering to teach him about the stars in return. The bargain was made and soon the music and astronomy lessons were in full swing. Mr. Eddowes was so impresesd with Joseph's teaching skill that he spoke of it quite freely, with the result that Joseph was asked to open a school for the children of his congregation. Besides the usual reading and writing, Joseph, with his persistent love of experimenting, introduced a small air pump and an electric machine bought in London with money earned through his classes. At first there was mild opposition to these as being too worldly, but Joseph preached a sermon on the miracles of Christ, and pointed out that the sparks created by the electric machine, and the vacuum created by the air pump were not worldly at all, but divine miracles and proof of God's power. He emphasized this in the case of electricity by pointing out that only a few years before, Benjamin Franklin in the American colonies had shown that electricity and lightning were identical.

The experiments with the electric machine proved most entertaining to the children and their parents. It was a crude affair consisting of a glass ball rotated by a hand crank on a rubber mat. As the electric force was generated, it was carried by a series of metal points to a prime conductor and, in some cases, the electricity was discharged in a sensational shower of sparks. When a bunch of hairs was held close to it, each hair stood out separately. The audience was much impressed.

The air pump interested Joseph more than the electric machine. Ever since his childhood when he had wondered about fish dying in air and spiders dying without it, he had been fascinated by the element that surrounded everything.

The experiments that he did with the air pump were the usual things. A vacuum was created in the round glass vessel, and the effect of the lack of air was noted on various objects such as a tube of mercury, a candle flame, or a mouse.

Joseph became so interested in teaching that when, in 1761, he was asked to teach languages at Warrington Academy which had recently been established, he accepted at once although he was quite happy at Nantwich. He had a struggle with his conscience about giving up his preaching, but he told himself that he would be learning by teaching, and if he preached occasionally he would feel more sure of himself in consequence. Warrington appealed to him especially after his first talk with Mr. Taylor, the headmaster.

"I'm glad to have you here, Mr. Priestley," Mr. Taylor said. "Word of your insistence on finding the truth has reached us up here. Both Mr. Ashworth of Daventry, and Mr. Meadows at Needham are friends of mine, and—well —I think you shocked them a little. Here at Warrington we believe that Dissenters should stand firm in liberty, and think and judge for themselves. I think we'll get along."

Warrington Academy was not restricted to religious teaching, and Joseph soon found himself asked to teach a variety of subjects from philosophy to anatomy. His profession of minister was put aside for the new interest in education. His active mind was filled with radical ideas as to what should be taught, and since his stammering was still somewhat of a handicap, he began putting his ideas into writing. Books with formidable titles flowed from his pen. Although scarcely twenty-nine years old, he wrote of history, government, oratory and civil liberty with the confidence of an expert. *The Theory of Language, Oratory and Criticism*, and *A Course in Liberal Education* were produced especially for his students, and *An Essay on Government*, and *A Chart of Biography* were written for the general public and published by the printer, J. Johnson, in London.

His skill in writing came to the attention of a former Warrington boy who was a student at Edinburgh University, Dr. Henry Percival. He showed a copy of Joseph's *Chart of Biography*, a summary of all the great names in history arranged according to dates and special fields of accomplishment, to the authorities, and persuaded them to grant Joseph Priestley a degree of Doctor of Laws.

"People will listen to you more," Dr. Percival said, laughing, "if you have a title in your name. I guarantee that Dr. Priestley will outdo Mr. Priestley a hundredfold. Mark my words."

In his classes at Nantwich, Joseph had had a young student, William Wilkinson, whose home was near Warrington. When the boy came home for a visit it was natural that he should see his old teacher, and Joseph became a frequent visitor at the Wilkinson house. Besides William, there was also Mary, a daughter. Since his mother's death Joseph had never known anyone with whom he felt particularly intimate. Mary Wilkinson was a great reader, an active and capable girl, and she and Joseph found a great deal in common. It wasn't long before they decided to be married. The wedding was a very quiet one, marred by

only one slight incident. The Reverend Thomas Thorkwald, who was to give Mary away, her father being absent
on business in Wales, fell asleep in his study just before
the ceremony and had to be awakened by the distraught
groom.

The couple set up housekeeping in part of a house near
the academy, and Joseph went on with his teaching, writing and studying.

He was still an ardent advocate of freedom of religious
thought, so much so that, in order to add strength to his
opinions, he became an ordained minister just before his
marriage. Nevertheless, ever since Mr. Hogue had mentioned the "wonderful things God has created for us" he
had concentrated more and more on learning all he could
about the natural things around him. He had read Gravesande's *Natural Philosophy* at Batley, and since then he had
spent many hours poring over every book on science on
which he could lay his hands.

One book especially impressed him. It was called *Elements of Chemistry*, one of the most comprehensive chemical treatises of the time, written just before Joseph was
born by a Herman Boerhaave, the son of a Dutch minister
at Leyden.

From it Joseph learned that the science of chemistry,
first so-called by Paracelsus in the sixteenth century, was
coming more and more into its own. The ancient Egyp-
tians and Chinese had called it alchemy, but their interest
in it was chiefly to find ways of turning base metals into
gold, which was considered the purest metal. Over the
years since the time of Paracelsus more and more men

39

were experimenting with metals, gases, vapors, fire and common air. At the end of the sixteenth century Andrea Libau analyzed the mineral water at Pyrrmont, Germany, and determined that it contained what he called "fixed air." In 1590 Jan van Helmont distinguished between gases and vapors, pointing out that vapors became liquid when exposed to cold—like the steam from a kettle, Joseph thought to himself. About the same time David Sennet and Joachim Jungius had defined the basic chemical element, calling it variously atom or corpuscle, as a substance in nature that could not be further decomposed.

Robert Boyle, whose life covered practically the whole of the seventeenth century, appealed especially to Joseph. Boyle insisted on experimenting in chemistry to find out all about metals, air and liquids. He was neither an alchemist seeking for gold nor a doctor looking for cures for sickness. To Joseph, this was the proper approach.

Boyle and a contemporary, Johann Becher, both detected the close relation between the burning of some substance and the loss of breath in a human being. Both men felt that in the case of burning or breathing there was a mysterious substance in the material burned or in the breath given off which caused it to be consumed. Boyle called it "fire substance," and Becher "fat earth." Later in the eighteenth century, about the time of Joseph's birth, Georg Ernst Stahl called it "phlogiston" from the Greek word *phlox* or flame. Joseph was much intrigued by this phlogiston theory of burning or combustion and ordinary human breathing or respiration. It seemed to him quite logical, and a sound explanation of the disappearance of anything that was burned or consumed. He stored it away in his mind as a basic truth.

Filled with enthusiasm over the efforts and findings of the men of past centuries, Joseph was overjoyed when Matthew Turner, a chemistry professor from Liverpool, gave a series of lectures at Warrington. He haunted Turner's classroom, taking copious notes and asking innumerable questions. Much that he heard he had learned already from his reading, but he was constantly on the alert for new ideas.

The four basic elements of the ancients: earth, air, fire and water, he learned, were being carefully investigated by men from different countries—Jean Hellot of France, Heinrich Pott of Germany, Antoinio de Ulloa of Spain and Richard Watson of England. The earth had been found to be made up of several different minerals including, of course, the gold that the alchemists were constantly talking about making out of something else. Fire was still rather a mystery and it was noted that the vapor from a kettle of boiling water disappeared into combination with the air.

"Among the various elastic fluids," Turner said, "is common air. We breathe it. We are completely surrounded by it. It is now assumed that this air which was thought to be made up of three elements: ordinary atmosphere, fixed air and inflammable air, may combine with many substances. The most important is what we call phlogiston. We are not sure yet if phlogiston and fire are the same, but we do know that phlogiston is the element which causes bodies to burn."

41

The lecturer then placed a burning candle in a closed vessel. The flame soon died down and went out.

"You see," Turner said with a confident gesture of the hands, "it is obvious that the air has become so saturated with the phlogiston from the candle that it can contain no more, and the flame goes out."

Turner may have been confident, but Joseph was not. He noted that many things were assumed by the lecturer. Water, which was held to be a single element, turned into a vapor and disappeared into the air when heated. This did not seem to be consistent with its being a single element. Again, Turner said that air might be made up of many substances, although he mentioned only three. This assuming of things was not Joseph's way, and he decided then and there that if the air were made up of a number of things he would find out what they were, and if water could be decomposed, he would try to do it.

He looked at the lecturer's desk. It was crowded with tubes of all shapes and sizes, kettles, retorts and glass containers of every kind. He knew that they cost a great deal of money, but he would have to get some of them. He was being slightly better paid now and decided to put all he could into whatever chemical equipment he needed. The only place to buy such things was in London, and that was two hundred and fifty miles away, but Joseph was stubborn. He persuaded Dr. Turner to go with him to help pick out what he needed, and engaged two seats on the Liverpool-London "Flying Coach."

Chapter Five

The Flying Coach picked them up in Warrington. There were not many passengers and Joseph sat on top with the coachman. He enjoyed the ever-changing scene as the coach rolled through village after village behind its team of four powerful horses. Occasionally at a stop for a change of horses, he would move inside to get a little sleep. The weather was generally good and the coach was able to average forty or fifty miles in a day, and except for one broken axle there were no untoward incidents. Joseph was secretly rather sorry that they didn't meet any highwaymen, as he had always wondered how he would act in such an emergency, but this was an experiment he had no opportunity to make.

On the fifth day the coach rattled over the cobblestones of London, and up to Batman's London Coffee House on Ludgate Hill. Joseph and Matthew Turner were hungry and tired, but a generous joint of veal washed down with a hot spiced wine, plus the comfort of a clean bed, took care of these troubles. Joseph was up early the next morning eager to explore. He walked by St. Paul's Church to the river's edge and back up the hill, pausing for a moment in the courtyard of Newgate Prison to gaze at the poor condemned prisoners in their iron-barred cells. It brought back vividly his childhood horror at the story in *Pilgrim's Progress* of the man in the iron mask who would never know salvation. It was a dismal sight, and he hurried back to the Coffee House in time to join Dr. Turner at break-fast.

"I have good news for you, Joseph," was Turner's cheery greeting. "You've heard, of course, of Dr. Franklin?"

Joseph had heard of Benjamin Franklin during his first year at Daventry in 1752. It was then that the gifted American printer, editor and scientist made his famous experiment with a kite, proving the direct connection between lightning and electricity, and thereby winning world-wide recognition. In fact it was this that had inspired Joseph to buy the electric machine for his classes at Nantwich. He nodded in answer to Turner's question.

"Well, since he came to London in connection with some colonial business," Turner went on, "he has founded a little society known as the Whig Club. The members are men of all sorts who have rather, shall we say, advanced ideas—which should appeal to you. They meet here at this Coffee House and, luckily enough, I know one or two of the members. If you'd like to meet the old man, I think we could join them." There was no hesitation in Joseph's answer.

The day passed quickly. Dr. Turner knew all the shops where they sold chemical apparatus, and since Joseph had only a limited amount of money, their errands were soon done and arrangements made for sending the purchases to Warrington by mail coach.

The Whig Club met in an upper room of the Coffee House and was presided over by Dr. Franklin. He was twice Joseph's age, but no sooner had they been introduced than Joseph sensed a feeling of mutual understanding. At first the talk was general. The vital news of the day was discussed. There was a growing threat of war with Spain coming on the heels of the English victory over France in the American colonies. It was all intensely interesting to Joseph since the members present were all men of the highest standing in their own fields. There was Richard Price, a leading theologian and political philosopher; John Canton, the physicist and experimenter in electricity, and many others whose names Joseph recognized.

It was through John Canton that the talk finally turned to electricity. Joseph was most anxious to hear the details of the famous kite experiment, but a little hesitant among the older men to bring up the subject. Finally his curiosity got the better of him.

"Dr. Franklin," he found himself saying in a pause in the conversation, "would I be presumptuous to ask you for some details of your experiment with the kite? One hears so many variations since news travels so slowly, and I'm afraid I have a passion for verifying facts."

Dr. Franklin turned to the younger man and smiled. "Dr. Priestley," he began, and his use of Joseph's newly acquired title of Doctor of Laws was most gracious and warmed Joseph's heart, "one need not be afraid of such a passion. I have it myself, and that is one reason why I made the experiment about which you ask."

The group around the table, somewhat startled by Joseph's question, now turned an attentive ear to their chairman.

"You may remember," Franklin went on, "that a Frenchman named Dalibard had, unbeknownst to me, ascertained that the lightning in the sky was identical with electricity. It is strange how similar ideas occur to men so far distant from each other. I had pondered over the possibility for some time and was, in fact, waiting for the building of a high spire in Philadelphia. There was some absurd delay in the course of construction, and I decided to go on alone. My problem was to get as far as possible into the sky."

"Wouldn't a pointed rod of a moderate height have been sufficient?" Joseph asked.

There was a slight note of irritation as Franklin answered. "You are speaking, Dr. Priestley, through knowledge acquired *since* my experiment. Remember, men were not sure that the earth was round until they sailed around it."

Joseph realized that he had been impetuous, but he also knew that it was his nature to be when in search of facts.

"I solved this problem," Franklin went on, "by the use of a kite with a steel key attached to the cord near my hand. I chose a day when the air indicated the approach of a storm, and—"

"What material did you use for the kite?" Joseph asked. There was a stir among the other listeners, but Joseph was fearless now. He wanted a clear picture and he would settle for no less. This time Franklin showed no sign of irritation. He seemed to recognize the zeal of a fellow experimenter.

"I should have mentioned that," he answered. "I used a large silk handkerchief spread on two long cross-sticks. I persuaded my son, who was then a lad of about twenty-five, to help me. Frankly, gentlemen, I was a little afraid of public ridicule should the experiment fail. Together we raised the kite a considerable distance into the heavens—and waited. I was just beginning to feel that my fear of ridicule was justified when I noticed that some of the loose threads of the hempen string were standing erect, appearing to avoid each other."

"Like the hairs near the prime conductor in the electric machine," Joseph put in enthusiastically.

"Exactly," Franklin agreed, "and to prove it was an electric charge, I applied my knuckles to the key at the end of the cord, and—" he extended his hands with a final gesture, "that was it. I experienced the tingle that comes only with a true electric contact. I had proved my point."

Joseph thanked him, the talk became again rather general and by ten o'clock, after a final round of hot spiced wine, "a good negus," as Franklin called it, the company broke up.

"You seem vastly interested in natural philosophy, Dr. Priestley," Franklin remarked as they said good night. "What brings you to London?"

Joseph explained his recent enthusiasm for chemistry and expressed a hope that he might have the pleasure of seeing Dr. Franklin again.

"I presume that you must be getting back to Lancashire for your teaching," Franklin replied. "Shall we have a talk tomorrow?" This was more than Joseph had hoped for, and it was quickly arranged that they would meet the next day at Franklin's lodgings on Craven Street.

When they met, the talk began with a discussion of the

47

broad field of natural philosophy, as science in general was then called. An idea occurred to Joseph and at the first opportunity he broached it.

"Has there ever been a book written on the history of electricity?" he asked.

"Not that I know of," Franklin answered. "Why don't you write one?" he added with a smile. This was just the idea Joseph had in mind, but he was flattered at the suggestion coming so promptly.

"I'm afraid," he replied, "that my knowledge of the subject is very limited. I should have to read a great many books, and—"

"I know," Franklin interrupted, "and books are expensive, but I think I could help out there. I have with me quite a number on the subject, and my friend John Canton can supply you with others." He leaned back in his chair. "It's quite an idea. I'd like to see you do it."

Since Joseph was not one to refuse a challenge, he agreed to work on the book. The talk shifted to American affairs. The year was 1765. George III was keeping a heavy hand on his colonies in America, giving them orders about their trade, imposing tax after tax and keeping his soldiers active in enforcing all his unwelcome laws. There was growing discontent in America, and Franklin, as a representative of the province of Pennsylvania and deputy postmaster for all provinces, was deeply concerned.

"England is being too severe," he said. "Mark my words, American men will stand just so much and then they will protest."

Joseph listened attentively. Here, he thought to himself,

was a third world, the world of men. It seemed to complete the picture—God, nature and now men. He must look into it, but first things first. He had a history of electricity to write.

Back in Warrington a few days later, Joseph lost no time in beginning work on the history. He very carefully organized his regular lectures and classes, allotting time for writing. Mary smiled at his enthusiasm. It was one of the reasons she loved him. Nothing must interfere when Joseph started on a project, and she carefully reorganized the work of the house. Small as it was, she contrived a room for a laboratory. The chemistry apparatus was put aside for the moment, and the electrical machine installed in a place of honor. Joseph's first task was to read the books given to him by Franklin and Canton. They were interesting and Joseph could easily have merely summarized them, but that was not his way. Statements had to be verified by experiment, and new ideas growing out of them must be investigated.

Joseph promised himself that he would finish the book in a year and then get back to his chemical studies. When he had first listened to Matthew Turner talk about chemistry, the world of religious debate had suddenly seemed rather futile. One could not really change people. They either disagreed and hated you like the congregation at Needham, or they were indifferent and not worth wasting words on like the Nantwich group. The world of nature, chemistry and electricity was based on facts. One had only to find these facts, and that was that. No arguing.

One might be wrong at first about the facts, but there was little room for opinion after sufficient experimentation.

Starting with almost no knowledge of the subject, Joseph pored over the books given him by his friends, and then wrote seven hundred pages of his own. He covered the whole span of the subject, starting with the Greek Thales of Miletus who, six hundred years before Christ, first rubbed a piece of amber, known in his language as *electros*, and found that it attracted other small objects. He dealt with William Gilbert who in the early seventeenth century spoke of the similarity between cohesion, or the sticking together of particles of matter, and magnetism. Much space was given to Isaac Newton who, toward the end of the seventeenth century, made a study of the attraction of bodies toward the earth and determined a formula for this force. Electricity, Joseph pointed out, was a fluid that existed in all bodies of matter in a certain proportion. If for any reason a body lost some of its electric fluid, it was said to have positive electricity, and if it gained more than the normal amount it had negative electricity. These terms had first been used by his friend Franklin, although the existence of two characteristics of electric fluid had been known for some time.

He had chapters on the Leyden jar, which was simply a glass container or condenser which was found to hold a charge of electricity for a long time or until discharged. It was invented by a Dutch minister in the town of Leyden about 1740.

The more he found out, the more he wanted to know, and he made innumerable experiments of his own. He was testing the conductivity—or the power of transmitting electric fluid—in a variety of substances like charcoal, slate, marble and chalk, when he thought to try the flame of a candle. He brought the flame between two brass knobs, one touching the inside of his Leyden jar, and the other the outside. As he brought the flame toward the knobs it quivered and was drawn both ways, leaving the wick bare on top. When it was directly between the knobs, the Leyden jar or battery discharged at once. The candle flame was undoubtedly a conductor of electricity.

In one of his many talks with Franklin he had learned that his friend had found that currents of air appeared to come from projecting points on conductors which had received a shock of electricity. This was enough for Joseph. He recalled that it had often been noticed that when lightning struck, people nearby had actually been thrown down but were not burnt or hurt. Hearing of Franklin's experiment, he saw the similarity and decided to try and prove it. He found that a piece of cork or some other light object placed near a condenser was moved some distance when the condenser or jar was discharged. He then went still further and connected several jars together to make the discharge stronger. When the same cork was placed in the same position, he found that the discharge of one jar moved it one fourth of an inch, two jars one inch and a quarter, and three jars one inch and three quarters. Little wonder, he thought, that such a large discharge as lightning would move heavy bodies a considerable distance without actually charging them with electricity.

Often Joseph would conduct an experiment and describe it in his book, even though he was not able fully to explain it. One day he decided to try a spark jumping a gap in a vacuum. He pumped the air from a glass container in which there were two rods connected with the inside and the outside of his condenser. He varied the gap between the rods and the spark continued to jump it when the condenser was discharged. When the gap reached two inches a remarkable thing happened. Joseph had accepted the usual rule that electricity passed in one direction from positive to negative. To his amazement, when the rods were two inches apart, the gap was suddenly bridged by a thin blue or purple light. It was quite uniform in appearance and there was no perceptible difference between the two terminals as there would have been in an ordinary discharge. It was evident to Joseph that the electric fluid was going and returning in the same path with incredible speed, an oscillatory current, back and forth like a pendulum. He had never heard of such a thing and was quite unable to explain it. There seemed to be no difference here between positive and negative electricity. This electric fluid, he thought to himself, is certainly the most mysterious thing in science. Maybe someday we'll have the answers, and even possibly some practical use for it. Had he been able to look ahead a hundred years he would have seen the Italian inventor Guglielmo Marconi using this very oscillatory principle in wireless telegraphy.

While working on these lateral explosions, as he called the indirect force of an electric shock, Joseph had occasion to transmit the shocks through a piece of brass. He noticed that wherever the current went through the brass and melted it, there was a distinct circle, the outer edge of which appeared greenish. He tried to wipe off this color with his finger but he made no impression on it. He then examined the odd new circle through a microscope, and to his surprise he found that all the colors of the spectrum were there in the order of the rainbow. The first, or red, was about a third of an inch, and the last, or violet, about one fourth of an inch. He repeated the experiment thirty or forty times with a resulting ring of about one inch in width. He brought Mary in and showed the rings to her.

"They are sort of like the fairy rings," Mary suggested, "that we sometimes see in the meadows. There is a super-stition, you know, that they are caused by lightning."

"Some sign from God, perhaps," Joseph added. "At least the lightning comes from the direction of Heaven. It's a pleasant thought, Mary."

Chapter Six

In July of 1767, barely a year after he started work, Joseph gave the manuscript to Johnson, the printer, in Temple Bar, London. While it was being prepared, Joseph received a letter from Franklin telling him of a recent experiment of his own.

Dear Joseph,

I congratulate you on finishing the history. It should be a great contribution to science.

The other day I enclosed two pith balls in a metal vessel which I had previously charged with electricity. I was astounded to find that the two balls remained totally unelectrified. Why don't you put your versatile mind to work on this? Let me know what you come up with.

Your friend

B. Franklin

This was enough to set Joseph to work. By rotating his electric machine he electrified a tin quart vessel which he stood on a stool of baked wood. He then hung two small balls, made from the pith of elder, by threads to the end of a glass stick so that they and the threads were entirely within the vessel. To his surprise, the balls remained completely untouched by any electric force. He had verified Franklin's experiment, but what was the reason? To Joseph, that was all important. Night after night he lay

awake trying to solve the problem. Then the answer came
quite unexpectedly. With his usual care he was putting
away his notes for the *History of Electricity* when he
came upon those for his chapter on Isaac Newton and the
gravitational theory. He read at first casually and then with
sudden interest, "so it is undoubtedly true that were the
earth in the form of a shell, a body in the inside of it would
not be attracted to one side of it more than another." This
must be it. He read it again. The conditions were identical.
This must be the answer. Gravity was identical with electric attraction, and therefore the two pith balls remained
untouched by any force in the surrounding walls of the
vessel. It was a tremendous idea and he wrote of it in a
letter to Franklin.

"—and if we carry the idea further, we are justified in
applying Newton's law of gravitational attraction to electricity, and saying that electrical attraction between bodies
is in inverse square to the distance between them."

Before this letter was answered, Joseph repeated his
remarks to Lord Henry Cavendish, a well-known English
scientist and a member of the Whig Club. He and Joseph
were about the same age and frequently talked over their
experiments. Cavendish was delighted with the idea. "Do
you mind if I make a final test?" he asked.

Joseph never objected to the most careful testing of his
ideas, and he watched with interest as Cavendish prepared
to test this new one in another way. Taking a twelve-inch
globe covered with tin foil, he carefully insulated it. Then
he placed around it two pasteboard hemispheres in such
a way that no part touched the globe. He electrified them

from a Leyden jar, connected them for a moment with the inner sphere by a wire and then removed them. Two pith balls were suspended near the sphere. The two men watched anxiously. They knew that if the spheres had become charged, the pith balls would react to the electricity. There was not the slightest movement. It was apparent that no charge had passed from the highly electrified hemispheres, and the similarity to gravitational force was quite evident.

"It's revolutionary, Priestley," Cavendish said quietly. "You seem to have hit on a sure basis for measuring the force of electric fluid. We simply apply the laws of gravitational force to electricity."

The answer from Franklin was equally heart-warming.

Your new theory of the measurement of electricity is most ingenious. I don't see how you do it. In an amazingly short time you have added more to our knowledge of electricity than many men I know with twice your training in science. You should be one of the most prolific contributors to the reports of the Royal Society.

Your friend

B. Franklin

Experiment followed experiment. He took nothing on faith. He showed conclusively that carbon was a good conductor, and ice and red-hot glass fair. He measured the obstruction presented to an electrical discharge from the length of wire forming the circuit by measuring the air gap across which a spark would pass in preference to going all the way through the wire circuit. He found this to be proportional to the length and inversely proportional to the square of the thickness of the wire used. In all cases he repeated his experiments—sometimes as many as fifty times—to be sure there was no error. He was thoroughly enjoying himself.

In the meantime Mrs. Priestley was having her problems. In 1763 a daughter was born. They were both delighted and agreed to call her Sarah after Joseph's aunt who had been so good to him and had only recently died. It was, however, one more in the family and consequently an increase in expense. As it was, Joseph's salary of a hundred pounds from his teaching was already stretched to the breaking point, even though they rented two rooms in their house to students at fifteen pounds a year. Joseph had to have a laboratory; money had to be spent on new equipment; and although Mrs. Priestley was thoroughly sympathetic and quite willing to take on extra work, it did make life extremely difficult. Secretly she wished he would go back to his work as a minister, but she loved him and was filled with much of his enthusiasm for science, so she said nothing and struggled on.

The *History of Electricity* finally appeared. Joseph need have had no fear of its reception. He received a letter from the Royal Society of London informing him that he had been elected a Fellow of the Society, not only because of the book but also on account of his extreme interest and skill in science. Joseph Priestley, the weaver's son, had come a long way.

Proud of his success with the first volume of the *History of Electricity*, Joseph was quite content in his work and the long hours of teaching matched by hours spent in the laboratory. He was prepared to spend the rest of his life in Warrington. Unfortunately, the practical problem of a growing family and money for their upkeep faced him daily. Furthermore, his wife was not in the best of health and, remembering the early death of his mother from over-work, he decided to make a move. The congregation at Leeds, only a short distance from his old home, was in need of a minister. They were known as very freethinking peo-ple, and the salary was better enough to make it pretty certain that his domestic problem would be partly solved. So, late in 1767 at the age of thirty-four, he moved with his family and his laboratory equipment to the town of Leeds as minister of Mill Hill Chapel. Until permanent quarters could be found, the Priestleys lived comfortably, if not elegantly, in a small house next door to a brewery.

To be neighbor to a brewery was upsetting to Mrs. Priestley, but Joseph discounted the social aspect of the situation and became deeply interested in the making of beer. He watched the men prepare the mash of crushed barley, rice, corn and water, and rotate it in a huge cask. What interested him especially was boiling this mash in a copper vessel. As it boiled, bubbles appeared on the surface that reminded him of those on the surface of a brook that had puzzled him so as a little boy. It set him to thinking. If the bubbles on the surface of the stream were filled with fresh or common air, should not these mash bubbles be filled with some other sort of air because of all the things that had gone into making it? No sooner did an idea occur to Joseph than he felt he must explore it, and he went into action at once.

The workmen at the brewery had become quite accustomed to seeing the reverend doctor watching them work. If this was the way their minister chose to spend his hours outside of church, it was certainly his own affair, and there was little or no comment. When, however, they saw a pair of black-stockinged legs on the rungs of a ladder leaning against one of the fermenting vats, they felt that the matter needed looking into. One of them climbed a nearby ladder and had a good look. He was down again in an instant, reporting that Dr. Priestley was undoubtedly the owner of the legs, and that the rest of him was leaning into the boiling vat, poking the bubbles as they rose to the surface with chips of wood which he lighted from a candle held in his hand. Considering the fact that only the Sunday before, Dr. Priestley had preached a fiery sermon on the dignity of a Christian, this was certainly strange conduct.

Joseph, meanwhile, ignored the not very complimentary remarks that drifted up to him on his precarious perch. He was learning that as a bubble broke, the air inside it instantly put out his burning chip of wood. It was evident that it was ordinary air, and that it had become impregnated with foreign substances from the boiling mash. He must, he decided, collect some of it and test it in his own laboratory. This was a very slow process and he returned day after day, collecting a little at a time in bladders. When he had a substantial quantity, he first tried its solubility in water. He found that it was reasonably soluble, some of it rising to the surface as bubbles. He sniffed the mixture and found it quite odorless. Then, although it was a risky thing to do, he tasted it. It was pleasantly sweetish and reminded

59

him of the natural spring water from Nieder Seltzer in Germany that he had once tasted. Was it possible that he had hit on an artificial water that might have all the curative effects of the natural Seltzer water? It was an exciting idea, and he decided to report his findings to the Royal Society in London.

First, however, he had to have a much larger quantity than he had been able to collect laboriously from the copper vats in balloonlike bladders. This was the common method, but it was clumsy. Surely, Joseph thought, there must be a better way. If only he could produce the same thing in his own laboratory, he could collect a much greater amount. The problem was to find the right ingredients for the new air and a better way of collecting it. He remembered that his friend Cavendish, some few years before, had written a paper describing what he called "factitious air" which he defined as "any kind of air which is contained in other bodies in an elastic state, and is produced from thence by art." This seemed to describe the air from the mash pretty well. Cavendish had produced a form of factitious air, which he called fixed air, by the use of acid on an alkaline substance, and Joseph decided to begin by trying the effect of vitriolic acid on chalk. The resultant gas he passed through a trough of water into an inverted bottle, which proved to be a much less laborious method than using bladders. When he had collected quite a quantity he tested it just as he had the air from the vats. To his delight he found that the taste and appearance were identical.

Trips to London had become a regular routine, and on his next visit he took a bottle of his precious water to a regular meeting of the Royal Society. He explained what he had done, and at the request of the president, Sir John Pringle, he performed the experiment before the membership. He was a new member, and he felt a little hesitant at first. Perhaps the experiment might not work; after all, he hadn't tried it as many times as was his custom.

All eyes were on him as he arranged his equipment. He put a bowl of water on a table. Then he filled a narrow glass vessel with water, and by placing a piece of soft leather on top, he inverted it in the bowl, thus assuring that no outside air would get in. He then placed on a lower table a narrow-necked bottle with not too finely powdered chalk and a little water. Into this he put a teaspoonful of oil of vitriol, corked the bottle and connected it by a flexible leather tube run through a bladder to the mouth of the vessel standing in water in the bowl. He carefully explained each move. As the gas rose from the chalk, he pressed the bladder, thus forcing the contents into the vessel. At first the air drove out the water, but almost at once, as the air became absorbed, the water rose until the vessel was filled.

The members were attentive, but they were not convinced that the water was really impregnated. Joseph turned to the president and held out the bottle of water.

"The proof lies in the taste," he said. "Would your Lordship care to prove the test?" Thus publicly challenged, the distinguished gentleman had to accept. He tilted the glass and sipped. There was a pause and then

Sir John took a long draught. Putting the glass down, he looked at Joseph with a smile.

"Very pleasant," he said, and the strain in the room was relieved by a shifting in seats and a clearing of throats. "It seems to me," he went on, "that this is identical with Seltzer water. Gentlemen, this is indeed an important discovery, and I move a vote of thanks to our young member, Dr. Priestley."

The applause was pleasant for Joseph, but better yet was a letter he received a month or so later when he had returned to Leeds. It was from the secretary of the Royal Society.

Dear Dr. Priestley,

I have been instructed to inform you that the Society was much impressed by your recent experiment in impregnating water with gas.

The matter was taken up with the College of Physicians, and pursuant to their favorable findings, the water was offered to the Lords of the Admiralty for use in the navy, its preventive effect in the matter of scurvy being deemed highly probable. The Right Honorable John, Earl of Sandwich, the First Lord Commissioner, will shortly be in touch with you.

May I add my own personal felicitations on your ingenuity. You have indeed made a contribution to the Empire's well-being.

With deepest respect
I am your humble servant
Lionel Cholmondeley
Secretary of the Royal Society
of London

Word of the honor that had been accorded their minister soon spread through the parish of Mill Hill Chapel. He began to be looked upon as a sort of miracle maker. His sermons were radical, and his stammering was by no means wholly cured, but the congregation was extremely freethinking, and they enjoyed his attacks on many of the forms and ceremonies of the High Church people. He became a thorn in the side of the government and the supporters of the legal Church of England. The King and Parliament, however, were having their troubles with the American colonies, and they didn't choose to add to their burden by taking action against this firebrand minister at Leeds. Besides, Joseph was acquiring a reputation as a scientist, and in this field he was above criticism.

One member of his congregation, a Miss Letitia Fallon, held firmly to the theory that the Reverend Dr. Priestley *was* a miracle worker. She lived alone, not far from the chapel, and was a most conscientious churchgoer, sitting regularly in the front pew where she had an unobstructed view of the minister conducting the service, and could hear every word of his sermons. Joseph might have been flattered by this admiring attitude, but unfortunately Letitia Fallon had a reputation for being somewhat "teched in the head."

One day Joseph was in his laboratory experimenting with his electric machine, attempting to heat substances by an electric charge rather than by means of his grate fire or the flame of a candle. He was so absorbed that he failed to hear his door open, or see a visitor enter the room.

"Dr. Priestley, you *must* help me!"

63

He turned in surprise to see a very much disheveled Letitia. Her eyes had a frightened look; her hair was down on her shoulders and her clothes were disordered as though she had been tearing at them. His first thought was that she had been attacked by a robber, but knowing her appearance and financial circumstances he discounted this, and helped her to a chair. She was trembling and muttering to herself.

"Control yourself, Letitia," he said soothingly, "and tell me what's troubling you."

She gasped and swallowed hard. "It's the Devil, Dr. Priestley."

This was such a broad statement that Joseph was at a loss to know just what sort of sympathy he should express, and he said lamely, "The Devil, Letitia?"

Letitia nodded excitedly, grasped Joseph's hand and put her forehead on it, sobbing. "He has me in his power. He is tearing at me from inside. You must help me—you must —you must."

Joseph pushed her gently back in her chair and wiped his hand on his coattail. Letitia was perspiring. He gave her a glass of water and finally got her quieted down.

She spoke in a half whisper. "He got into me this morning, Dr. Priestley. What have I done to deserve this? You are a man of God. I came to you right away. You must drive him out. Who else but you could?"

"The Devil," Joseph suggested, "cannot stand kind thoughts. Try to be calm and think of all your friends and all the beauties of the world. Think of Christ and His miracles."

64

Letitia was silent for a moment, trying hard to follow her minister's advice. She was trembling and finally, shaking her head, she looked up at Joseph pathetically, "It's no use. He won't leave me. You've got to help me, Joseph."

The use of his first name, so unlike the usual Letitia, made the appeal seem desperately personal. He had never before been asked to exorcise the Devil, and furthermore, he had never considered it to be one of his duties. He smiled to himself as he thought back to the days of Amos Woburn, who had told him that the Devil was in him. Something had to be done, but what? As he was thinking, his eye fell on the electric machine with which he had been experimenting when Letitia came in. He thought to himself, why not give her a jolt with an electric current? It could do no harm, and it might just frighten her enough to make her forget the Devil idea.

"Miss Letitia," he said kindly, "perhaps we can get rid of this Devil. Will you do exactly as I say?"

She nodded helplessly, and Joseph hastened to set up his equipment. He planned to use her as the prime conductor, and then by a quick discharge give her a violent shock.

The setup was very simple and Letitia was quite cooperative. He placed her on an insulated stool and gave her the end of a small chain attached to the prime conductor. Then he began turning the glass ball against the rubber mat, carefully watching Letitia. She winced as the current began tickling her, and looked pleadingly at Joseph. He smiled encouragement, turned the crank a little faster and then touched her with a conductor. There was a sudden spark. Letitia let go the chain she was holding, gave a little

65

scream and fell in a heap at his feet. Joseph helped her to a chair and sat holding her hands for some moments. Letitia sighed a very deep sigh and looked at Joseph without speaking, as though waiting for some demonstration from the Devil. Apparently there was none, for a smile spread over her face as she leaned toward him and said in a delighted whisper:

"He's gone, Joseph, he's gone. I knew you could do it."

Joseph was a very honest man, and his ideal was the truth, but he felt that in this case an exception should certainly be made.

Chapter Seven

Joseph's work with electricity had left him barely any time for chemistry. His experience in the brewery that had turned out so satisfactorily brought back his enthusiasm, and he began experimenting again. From his earliest childhood, air had always interested him, and he concentrated his efforts on it. He reasoned that it could not be, as was generally supposed, a single element or, at the most, three. So much in the way of evaporating liquids, smoke and human and animal breath went into it constantly and disappeared. These must, he felt sure, put various elements into the common air that men breathed.

Then there was the phlogiston that Dr. Turner had mentioned in his lectures that led to his meeting with Franklin. According to this theory, phlogiston was an element contained in all substances that could burn. The name was first used by Georg Stahl in 1669, and ever since reading about him, Joseph had idolized him and his theories. Stahl maintained that as soon as the material was consumed by fire, all the phlogiston was taken out of it and absorbed into the surrounding air, which therefore became phlogisticated. Joesph had enthusiastically accepted this theory of fire and combustion in general, and it added to his conviction that the air might easily be made up of an infinite number of different elements. With his *History of Electricity* out of the way, he made it his goal to set up an efficient laboratory and find out all about these "airs," as he began calling them.

He moved his family to a better house nearer the chapel, and set up what he hoped would be a permanent laboratory. All his life he had been moving about from place to place, but this, he told Mary, would be their final home. The laboratory was small but quite complete enough for his immediate needs. He had the usual glass vessels for confining air, and had recently acquired a large earthenware trough, the sort commonly used for washing linen, and with it he devised his own method of collecting air. His general procedure, which he had used in the case of the charged water, was to fill one of the glass vessels with water, place a piece of soft leather over the mouth, upend it in water in his trough and remove the piece of leather. Then any air, from whatever source, he would lead by a leather tube through the water to the open end of the vessel. This air would then replace a certain amount of the water and be strictly isolated for study. This method Joseph was quite proud of. It replaced the older, clumsy custom of collecting air in balloonlike bladders which had the added disadvantage of not being transparent.

During his experiment with the gas from which he had made his artificial Seltzer water, much of the air was naturally absorbed by the water. It occurred to Joseph that very possibly there were other airs or gases that were so thoroughly absorbed by the water in his vessels that none of it appeared for examination. Some way, he felt, should be found to investigate these other airs by not bringing them, if they existed, into contact with water. The bladder method he discarded at once. Why not, he thought, substitute mercury for the water in his trough and in the vessel, leaving everything else the same? No sooner thought of than tried. That was Joseph's way.

He had used oil of vitriol on chalk to produce the air with which he impregnated the water in his first experiment, and he decided to try the same on common salt. He prepared his trough in the usual way, using liquid mercury instead of water. He put the salt in a glass tube, poured on the vitriol, and let the fumes of air pass through the tubing, through the mercury and into the vessel containing more mercury. To his delight, the mecury was displaced by a great quantity of some sort of air. He inverted the vessel, after covering its mouth, and stood it on a table. Then he tested the air. It had a pungent, irritating smell unlike anything he had come across before. He repeated the experiment, using water, and found that the water absorbed the air so greedily that if he had conducted the experiment over water he would never have found it. He got some of the solution on his hand and it stung him. He took a cloth to wipe up some of the solution that had spilled on a metal rod that he used in his electric work. To his astonishment, the more he rubbed the metal, the brighter it became. When Mrs. Priestley heard of it she insisted that Joseph make up a supply for polishing anything made of metal around the house. It was so successful that instead of calling it "that stuff in the bottle," Joseph began speaking of it as "muriatic acid." He reasoned that it was the result of acid poured on salt, and the French word *muria* meant brine.

Any experiment like this Joseph reported to Franklin whenever they met in London, which they did more and more often. But they talked of many things besides science. Franklin was a Quaker, and his simple outlook in religious matters endeared him to Joseph; his interest in education which led him to found an academy in Pennsylvania was similar to Joseph's, and when he spoke at length, as he always did, about the troubles of the American colonies, Joseph was intrigued. America had been settled by Englishmen who wanted freedom to live and worship as they saw fit, and now George III was interfering with this freedom.

"There is a bitterness growing in America," Franklin said one day, "that people over here in England don't realize, but I think the future seems pretty dark. In 1763 the so-called Sugar Act that levied new duties on foreign goods and compelled the colonists to sell certain things only in England made people think; the Stamp Act that forced Americans to pay for stamps on all legal documents made people talk, even though it has been repealed. The next step is action, and I dread to think what that will lead to."

Rebellion against injustice, action to right a wrong— these things appealed to Joseph. However, he was so absorbed in his church work and his chemistry, he felt that there was no room in his life for any other activity. Then a series of events occurred that changed this point of view and, in some respects, his life.

On a Sunday late in 1770, Joseph preached a sermon on his favorite topic, the unity of the world under God. "All things," he said, "from the humblest growing things to the greatest works of man are merely manifestations of the all-embracing power of God." In a sense it was an explanation of his interest in electricity and chemistry which was causing many tongues to wag. There was much talk of all the bottles, machines and flasks that were seen in his house; and his climbing over the vats of mash in the brewery had not escaped attention and criticism, even after he was honored by the Royal Society. It was felt that this man of God was serving two altars.

"So there are two worlds," he said in conclusion, "in which we can worship God—religion and natural philosophy—one is no more or less important than the other."

The service ended, he started home, eager to get to work in his laboratory. He had so many experiments half completed.

"Excuse me, Dr. Priestley, may I have a word with you?"

Joseph looked up at a man who had caught up with him.

"My name," the stranger continued, "is Edmund Burke. You may, perhaps, have heard of me." He added this quite modestly, merely as a means of identification.

Joseph had indeed heard of him. He was the young, new member of the Irish Parliament who had been causing quite a stir in government circles by his criticism of England's attitude toward her American colonies and liberty in general.

"I enjoyed your sermon," Burke went on.

Joseph stopped a moment in surprise. "You were in the chapel just now?" he asked.

"Yes," Burke answered, and then smiled. "Oh, I can

understand your surprise. You have, I take it, heard that I am a Papist. My enemies call me all manner of things, and I pay no attention. Actually, I personally am a Presbyterian, although my wife is a Roman Catholic. I am on my way to London from Edinburgh. The coach broke down and—"

"And having nothing better to do, you dropped into our chapel," Joseph broke in with a laugh.

"Not exactly. I have heard your name in connection with your experiments in natural philosophy, and I have been anxious to meet you." They had reached Joseph's house and soon were seated in his laboratory.

"You made a good point in your sermon," Burke went on, "but I don't believe you went far enough."

Joseph felt that his statements had been pretty all-inclusive, in fact perhaps a little too much so, and he raised his eyebrows in surprise.

"I am, as you know, a politician," Burke explained, "but I am also a religious man, and as I view the present state of government, I feel that we are straying very far from any divine road. Politics is the managing of the affairs of people all over the world, and I feel that your thesis, while excellent, was not truly complete. You should have added to religion and natural philosophy the science of politics. It is a science, you know. After all, God made people as much as he made all the mysterious things you study."

The young Irish politician was putting into words the very thoughts that had been in Joseph's mind during his first talk with Franklin. The world of men was as much a part of God's plan as that of theology and science. He listened with his usual care to Burke's description of the highhandedness of George III, of the powers he granted to undeserving men in return for trifling favors, of the ignorance of the real needs of the masses of people, and the greedy accumulation of taxes at the cost of starvation. It was a dreary picture and quite out of line with God's teaching. Joseph's eager mind took it all in. It followed what Franklin had told him.

On his next visit to London, he made a point of visiting the House of Commons, and watched his new friend in action. The subject under discussion was the right to tax the American colonies, special debate being held over the question of the duty on tea imported from England which was causing riots and bloodshed in America. Young Burke did not disappoint Joseph. The benches were silent when he rose to speak. He was not an imposing figure, but being young and a new member he held a great interest for both the liberal, so-called, Whigs and the Royalist Tories, and they wanted to hear every word.

His smooth, effortless way of speaking was especially remarkable to Joseph, who was constantly in fear of stammering. There was a keen logic based on fundamental truth that appealed to him. After his personal talk with Burke, Joseph knew that in everything Burke said he was fighting to put English politics on a sure foundation of faith and Christian principles. He watched the slight, eager figure standing before the leader's chair fearlessly holding forth on all the things in which Joseph himself believed. He remembered Ben Franklin's warning that the American colonists were fighting for their liberty, and he resolved to join the fight and put as much energy into it as he had put into preaching and experimenting in science. He realized only too well that his congregation at Leeds would have a basis now for accusing him of serving not only two altars, but three—God, science and politics. If he could only show them that it was in reality the same altar—a universe of God's making.

Joseph was not one to delay, especially under pressure of conviction, and the Sunday after his visit to Parliament he rose before his congregation. He wasn't too sure of just what he was about to say. Perhaps the listeners would walk out on him as they had at Needham. Like all of his experiments, however, this had to be carried to a conclusion at whatever risk.

He took as his text the appearance of Christ before Pontius Pilate. Here, he pointed out, was the first contact of Christianity with the political world. Pilate released Barabbas and then washed his hands of responsibility in order to save his own position in the government.

"We here in England," he went on, "are not free of this unchristian attitude. It is growing and spreading like the Black Death. A very great majority of Englishmen, I am well persuaded, are friends to what are called high maxims of government. They would choose to have the power of the crown enlarged rather than reduced, and would rather see all of us Dissenters banished than any reformation made in the Church. A dread of everything tending to republicanism is manifestly increased of late years and is likely to increase still more. The clergy, the followers of Christ, have contributed not a little to the leaning to arbitrary power in the crown, which has lately been growing upon us. They preach the doctrine of passive obedience and nonresistance with little disguise, and their adulation of the King is abject in the extreme.

"This attitude is well shown in the treatment of England's American colonies. We, as Dissenters, have thousands of friends there—or, perhaps I should say, descendants of those who a hundred years or more ago fled from England to worship as they saw fit."

Joseph was deep in his subject now, as though it were some chemical experiment. He stammered only occasionally. The congregation was very quiet. He outlined the troubles in America, the protest against arbitrary taxes, and ended with a general plea for liberty.

"It must be understood, whether it is expressed or not, that all people live in society for their mutual advantage; so that the good and happiness of the members—that is, the majority of the members—of any state is the great standard by which everything relating to that state must be finally determined. Political liberty is a safeguard to civil liberty, which includes liberty of religious thought."

He had been addressing his own congregation in the privacy of their own chapel, but tongues wag and ears listen. It was not long before his sermon was the subject of debate in coffeehouses in nearby towns. It was discussed by passengers in coaches and thus carried to London. Members of Parliament heard of it over their "steaming negus" in their chosen coffeehouses or around dinner tables in their fashionable homes. From them it penetrated the Gothic walls of the Houses of Parliament and fell with

75

little grace on the ears of the Tories. It disturbed the sleep of the First Earl of Chatham, William Pitt, and even made the young king, George III, raise his eyebrows. On its flight, it came to the ears of William Fitzmaurice Petty, Second Earl of Shelburne, who held the proud office of Secretary of State to the Prime Minister. Lord Shelburne was a busy and a wealthy man with extensive estates in Wiltshire. He was a great reader, boasting of a rather unusual library at his country estate. He was a lonely man and held very radical ideas on a number of subjects. He heard what Joseph Priestley had said—and liked it. He had already heard about this fiery minister-chemist and his writing, and he sensed a chance to know him better. He found among his associates a mutual friend, and through him he wrote Joseph Priestley a letter.

The gist of it was that he had for a long time wanted someone to put his library in order, to help him with his Parliamentary paper work, to teach his son and to solace his own idle hours with literary discussion. The letter contained a definite offer of two hundred and fifty pounds a year in addition to forty for any expense he might be put to in pursuance of his scientific experiments, for which proper facilities would be provided.

The letter was a great surprise to Joseph, certainly a result of his sermon that he had not expected. There were many things in favor of accepting it. Two more children, Joseph Jr. and William, has been born during their stay in Leeds, and financial security for his growing family Joseph put first. There was also the prospect of a better laboratory than his makeshift one at Leeds, with the chance of new and exciting discoveries. The teaching, secretarial work and literary discussions should not be too arduous. He had promised Mary that the move to Leeds was to be the last, and any decision must be very carefully weighed.

While he was debating what to do, the situation was complicated by the receipt of another letter. It seemed that word of Joseph's contributions to science had reached the ears of James Cook, a lieutenant in the British Navy who had been assigned the task of plotting the transit of Venus and making general explorations in the South Seas. Cook invited Joseph to go along as spiritual and scientific adviser. Joseph was tempted. The prospect was full of interesting possibilities, but it had to be compared carefully with a life of experimentation in Shelburne Castle at Calne in Wiltshire. Then Fate stepped in and the decision was taken out of his hands. He received a second letter from the Cook expedition couched in the most flowery and polite terms, but saying, in effect, that it had been thought better to have someone whose spiritual views were somewhat more in accord with those of the Established Church of England, for fear the common seamen might be corrupted in their religious thinking.

Joseph had been used to this sort of thing from the time he was refused admission to his aunt's chapel, but the idea of his being actually a corrupting influence was bitter.

His wife knew how much he would have enjoyed the adventure of a scientific expedition. "Oh, Joseph," she said, "why do you have to oppose things so much?"

"I oppose only what is not the truth, Mary."

"But Joseph," she protested, "they say you might corrupt—"

Joseph interrupted her. "What they say, Mary, can't
hurt me. Remember, they are good Englishmen upholding
the laws of England. I am proud to be a good Christian,
and as such, I uphold the laws of Christ."

"Will you answer them?" Mary asked.

"I shall ignore them," Joseph replied, "and join Lord
Shelburne at Calne."

He tore the Cook letter into small pieces and dropped
them in the grate.

Chapter Eight

Joseph's resignation from the pulpit at Mill Hill Chapel was reluctantly accepted. Letitia Fallon was especially upset and demonstrated her sorrow in a vocal way that made Joseph doubt the value of his electric Devil-driving. The mysterious flasks, bottles and machines were loaded on the mail coach, an operation watched in wonderment by the many parishioners who had, up to that time, merely heard of the curious instruments used by their minister, and Joseph and his family followed in the regular coach. It was a tiresome journey as it was necessary to change coaches in London for the eighty-mile trip to Calne in Wiltshire, a few miles from the Shelburne estate. It was here that the contract called for Mrs. Priestley to set up housekeeping with the children, while Joseph was to spend the winter months at the castle or in London, and join his family for part of the summer. It was not the most satisfactory arrangement, but financial considerations precluded any argument. Calne lay in a rolling country of chalk hills very different from Yorkshire, and the Shelburne estate was hidden in its own park on the outskirts of the village.

Joseph settled his wife in comfortable rooms in Calne, hired a chaise and drove to "Bowood" as Shelburne's estate was called. As he drove up the winding road, he felt a little strange. He was entering a new life. He had changed around a good deal in his career, but his manner of life had not. The houses he had lived in had always been modest and unpretentious. Shelburne Castle was a triumph of the great architect Inigo Jones, a huge central building flanked by two long wings, dignified and classic in its lines, but softened and made hospitable by the setting of trees and shrubs.

Joseph found his duties as librarian very simple. The collection of books was interesting, but already fairly well organized. The young son Henry, a fragile, rather silent boy, was intelligent and responsive, a pleasure to teach. Joseph often commented about him to Mary, "I've never known a boy of such quick understanding." The daily conversations with his patron were anything but a chore; they were thoroughly enjoyable. Lord Shelburne trusted Joseph and talked very freely on political matters even when they involved himself. Joseph's own position was well known. It was what had drawn Shelburne's attention. Ever since his interest had been aroused by Franklin and Burke, Joseph had been talking in defense of the American colonies. In 1768 he published *The Present State of Liberty in England,* following it up with *Essays on the First Principles of Government.* These pamphlets were eagerly read by the enemies of George III.

The two men often talked far into the night. These conversations took Joseph away from his laboratory, but they also took him into his third world, that of politics, a world that was taking on greater and greater significance, especially the relations between England and her colonies. Lord Shelburne was a man with opinions of his own, with a fearlessness in expressing them, and he appealed to Joseph.

"You and I see eye to eye," Shelburne said one evening, "about the American colonists. It hasn't made me popular with our King George, I can tell you. He's stubborn as a mule and wants to rule his own way."

Joseph sensed the feeling of frustration in Lord Shelburne's voice.

"What do you think will happen?" he asked.

"Rebellion," was the prompt reply. "If you don't conciliate an aroused people, you must expect it. I've expected it ever since William Pitt spoke for conciliation—and how he could speak! The Great Commoner he was called. He believed in the rights of the common man—much as you do, Joseph. That's one reason I am glad to have you with me."

"If this taxation continues," Joseph agreed, "I'm sure you're right. Or else these three million colonists will be reduced to abject slavery."

Shelburne, who liked to see Joseph stirred up on any subject, delighted in goading him on. "What's the alternative?" he asked.

Joseph, as usual, was ready with an answer.

"As I said in my pamphlet, radical changes in the whole government system. We must think of the greatest good for the greatest number of our people. If this taxation is continued I shall take little account of my privileges as an Englishman and—" he paused and then reached into the world of religion for the end of his remark, "and think more of those that are infinitely more valuable—those of a Christian and a citizen of Heaven."

Lord Shelburne smiled. "I like that phrase, 'the greatest

good of the greatest number.' You are a powerful writer, Joseph."

A separate building on the estate had been set aside for Joseph's chemical work. It was a single room, but large and airy with a generous fireplace, grate and a good supply of coals and firewood. There were candles for light and the heating of retorts. It was, Joseph felt, ideal, and he was soon hard at work. He conducted a short service in Shelburne's private chapel on Sundays, but his ministerial duties gave way easily to the excitement of the laboratory.

He organized his single room with great care. It was a joy to have space enough to move around in. There was one long central table, and on this he stood his electric machine and air pump, and at the other end his most valuable tool, the large earthen trough filled with water that he used for collecting gases that were not soluble in water. It was deep at one end, but made shallow at the other by means of flat stones. He had contrived a cage for mice which he sometimes used for testing the breathability of the various airs. It was a glass jar open at the top and bottom, the bottom standing on a perforated tin plate raised an inch or two off the floor, and the top covered with a removable cap held in place by a weight. At the fireplace he had a gun barrel, the end of which he put into the hot grate to heat the contents. The resulting air he led from the end of the gun barrel to a bowl of mercury suspended from the mantel shelf. This in turn contained a narrow vessel also filled with mercury into which the air from the gun barrel was led, displacing the mercury.

So that he might carry on two experiments at once, he

had devised a mercury bowl similar to the one fed from the grate, but this one was fed from a glass tube containing the material and heated by a candle. When he wanted to impregnate water with some soluble air such as his fixed air, he did it by means of a bladder and a leather tube, forcing the air into a jar of water inverted over water by compressing the bladder. Besides the fire and the candle, he later used a large burning glass to concentrate the heat of the sun on the materials he was examining.

Every substance he heated seemed to give off an air with different properties. There seemed to be no end. Joseph used the word "air" for all of them, but as he found more and more airs, he began thinking of them as gases, the word used a hundred years before him by the Flemish chemist Jan Baptista van Helmont. He reasoned that if they mingled as they did with common air they could not be an integral part of it and therefore they should have a different name.

One thing puzzled him. The fact that so many gases mingled with the air, and so many animals either exhaled into it, or died and sent putrefaction into it, set him to wondering why the air he breathed was generally so pure. Any question to Joseph meant an experiment, and this certainly called for one. Besides, he had an idea. There were plenty of mice running around the castle, and Joseph caught several alive and put them in his mouse container. He then put one under a large bell jar and left it until it died, and the air was thoroughly putrid. He then carefully led this putrid air into two separate jars which were standing in water. In one he put a sprig of fresh mint from the garden, and waited several days. On the eighth day he took two of his mice, put one in the jar with the putrid air and the other in that containing the sprig of mint. The answer to his question came almost at once. The mouse in the jar with the mint moved about quite happily, but the poor creature in the other jar died in a few moments. It seemed apparent to Joseph that vegetation was not only pleasant to look at, but served in some mysterious way to purify air. Another proof, he felt, that God's plan was complete, that there was no separating religion and natural science.

Being methodical, Joseph kept a very careful record of the various substances he used, the acids he had mixed with them, and the resulting color, smell, solubility and amount of displacement when collected over mercury. It was to him a veritable miracle that so many different gases were possible. He tried the action of nitric acid on iron, and secured a gas which he called nitrous air; he heated copper with spirits of salt and called the resulting gas marine acid gas, and found that he got the same result from heating spirits of salt alone. What fascinated him was that one thing led to another. He found himself continually reaching for and peering over a new horizon.

This was the case when he began experimenting with ammonia water, a liquid distilled from coke in a retort. He heated this water in the section of gun barrel and thrust it into the red-hot coals of his grate. He carefully inserted a pipestem in the barrel, stirred up the coals and waited. Soon the gas began to pass through the pipestem up into the container standing in mercury. The crude joints were not too exact and some of the gas leaked out.

It had an irritating odor and made his eyes smart until he could hardly bear it, but he persisted. Soon he had a sufficient quantity stored over the mercury. From the smell he was convinced he had found a totally new gas. It reminded him a little of the gas he had secured by heating common salt with vitriolic acid and which he had later dissolved in water and called muriatic acid.

To see if by any chance they were the same, he decided to mix them. Obviously, he reasoned, if they were the same there would be no change. He carefully prepared the gas from vitriolic acid and common salt. Standing the two containers on the table, he punctured the cork in each one, allowing the gases to meet. This was the sort of moment that made Joseph's heart beat faster. Would anything happen?

What did happen, Joseph told Mary afterward, was more exciting than any passage in scripture which, for Joseph, was saying a great deal. As soon as the two gases met in the air a pure white cloud was formed which gradually settled on the table as a very fine white powder. Joseph leaned over and sniffed. There was no odor, and this seemed very strange since the two gases that formed it were both distinctly pungent. He touched the powder with his finger and tasted it. It was salty but not at all like the original salt. He sat staring at the little white pile. There must be some value to this new substance he had accidentally created. Perhaps if he tried heating it, he would develop still another gas, a combination of the two that had produced the powder. Perhaps if he dissolved it in water, if it were soluble, he would have a new acid.

He was thinking of other ways in which he might test the nature of the powder when the door opened suddenly and Henry, his pupil, came running in. He had been told repeatedly not to disturb Dr. Priestley in his laboratory, but since Joseph had a remarkable ability to concentrate, these orders had been almost consistently disregarded. This time, however, Joseph was irritated. The opening of the door not only brought Henry, but also a rather stiff gust of wind. The neat little pile of powder was blown in an irregular path across the table. Joseph instinctively reached out his hand, upsetting a flask of water which trickled the length of the powder, turning it into a white paste.

"Oh, I'm sorry, Dr. Joseph," Henry said, and was so definitely upset that Joseph's irritation vanished. "I'll just clean it up and make a fresh supply, Henry," he said smiling, and reached out his hand to start cleaning up. As his hand touched the paste, he drew it back suddenly. He felt a distinct electric shock, a rather strong one. He glanced along the streak of paste and saw that it led directly to the prime conductor of his electric machine which he had left fully charged on the opposite side of the table. Could this white powder be a conductor of electricity? He cleaned it up carefully, keeping the paste in a pottery vessel. Perhaps it was just the water. He recharged the prime conductor with the electric machine and tried the same thing with water. He felt a slight shock. When he added the paste which he had put aside, the shock was infinitely greater. There was little if any doubt that the white powder he had created from the two gases was an excellent conductor of electric fluid.

Henry had watched the whole proceeding with interest and had even tried touching the paste. "What are you going to call it, Dr. Joseph?" he asked.

Joseph hesitated. "Well, among other things it had salt and ammonia in it," he said thoughtfully. "How does ammonium chloride sound?"

Joseph didn't know it but this name was never to be changed, and generations following him were to use his ammonium chloride as the basic element in dry batteries.

In the spring of 1772 Joseph stood again before the membership of the Royal Society of London, the same group which had been so impressed by his invention of artificial Seltzer water. The members listened with interest as he told them of mixing nitric acid with iron and producing what he called nitrous air which could be used as a test for the breathability of any air; of his proof that certain vegetation has the quality of purifying air which has been fouled by animal breath; of his use of quicksilver, instead of water, to study gases which might dissolve in water; of his discovery of new gases and the solution of them in water such as muriatic acid, marine acid gas and ammonium chloride, the last with the power of conducting electricity.

The paper made such an impression on the members of the Royal Society that they voted Priestley the Copley medal, the highest award possible in their organization. The contents of the paper reached the ears of the French Academy of Science, and they honored Joseph by making him a foreign associate.

Chapter Nine

For heating the various substances with which he experimented, Joseph had always used either his open grate or a candle. He had often considered the possibility of utilizing the heat of the sun through what was known as a burning lens. It was, however, an expensive instrument, and in order to be of real, practical use, it would have to be quite large. It remained a possibility in his mind for some time, and then one day in 1774 a friend presented him with a powerful sixteen-inch lens with a twenty-inch focal length supposedly capable of very efficient heat concentration. He had been using, as a rather crude substitute, a large mirror, but being a reflecting instrument it was awkward to use.

Thrilled with this new source of heat, Joseph tried it out before attempting any further experimentation. To his delight he found that it generated enough heat to burn paper, cloth or even wood. His method was to place the solid substance in a glass bell jar, leaving an opening in the top to carry off any gas generated into his container. One of the difficulties with this method was that of weather—it could only be utilized on bright, sunny days. On dark days or at night he had to use other methods.

On Sunday, August 1, 1774, Joseph preached as usual in the Shelburne chapel. It was a powerful sermon but Lord Shelburne didn't seem too pleased over it. The government was passing through a bitter crisis in its relations with America, and Joseph said many things which Lord Shelburne felt should not be said in the presence of his servants even though he himself partially agreed with them. Joseph took for his text Christ's words on the Cross, "Father forgive them for they know not what they do," harsh words under the circumstances for a loyal Englishman to listen to. His congregation was small, but Joseph didn't spare them on that account. He spoke with the same fire to one as to a thousand.

After the service he noticed a distinct and rather reproving coolness on his Lordship's part, but he passed it off as he did most criticism when he felt that he was right, and hurried back to his laboratory and his burning lens. He had among the substances with which he experimented a red powder with the rather complicated Latin name of mercurius calcinatus per se. There was nothing new or startling about the powder; it had been easily obtained for years by heating pure mercury in air. Karl Wilhelm Scheele, a Swedish chemist, had fairly recently produced a gas from it which he called "empyreal air." After he had named it he promptly forgot all about it.

Being something rather common, Joseph picked it as a trial substance for his sixteen-inch burning lens. He placed a quantity of it under his bell jar so arranged that any gas that might be formed would pass through a leather tube and into a mercury-filled bottle standing in his mercury trough.

The sun was high and strong, and Joseph concentrated its heat on the powder in the bell jar. After a few moments

89

he noticed by the reduction of the mercury in his bottle that gas was being expelled very readily from the red powder. This new method of securing air, or gas, from solid matter was working well. It came so easily that Joseph filled three containers with Scheele's empyreal air. When he inverted the bottles and they stood on the table in front of him, he wondered whether this gas, which was not new and which had been disregarded by previous experimenters, was worth testing or even keeping. Near him on the table was a short, lighted candle. Rather idly he picked it up, fastened it to a piece of bent wire and, removing the top of one of the bottles, put the candle in, quickly replacing the top as tightly as possible to prevent any outside air from entering. The candle would, of course, go out or burn for only a few seconds.

To his astonishment, the flame of the candle became larger and burned with a white, intense brilliance such as he had never observed before. It was a veritable miracle. Doubting his own senses, he dropped a piece of smoldering charcoal into the second bottle. Instead of dying out to a black cinder, it crackled into a cloud of sputtering sparks. Still unbelieving, Joseph heated an iron wire red hot and held it in the third bottle of the mysterious gas. The dull red of the wire turned into a golden blaze. Joseph was nonplused. He had often seen a candle burn in enclosed air, but it always burned fairly naturally, slowly going out as the phlogiston was absorbed by the air. This new air or gas must be capable of absorbing an enormous amount of phlogiston. He had tried the experiment of putting a sprig of mint in thoroughly phlogiston-laden air, and the plant had seemed to purify the air, but here there was no plant. It was as though the air was purifying itself.

In talking it over with the local chemist, he learned that a doctor in Edinburgh University had recently used lime water to hold air in a bottle. He had noted that part of the air was absorbed by the lime water as a milky white substance, and that the remainder of the air was inert and lifeless. He had tried putting a candle in it and the flame had died out at once.

Joseph listened and thought. The Edinburgh doctor had determined that there were two gases in the air we breathed and that one was absorbed by lime water and the other quite lifeless. His own mysterious air was distinctly not lifeless, a candle had burned brilliantly in it. Did this indicate that there was a third gas in the atmosphere?

Joseph had an idea—just a suspicion, but it was worth a try. He took some lead and brought it to a very high heat in the open air. He watched it carefully. Gradually but very certainly, it began to turn a reddish brown until he had a pile of red powder. He put this in the bell jar and turned his burning lens on it as he had in the case of the mecurius calcinatus per se. He gathered the resulting gas in the three bottles, and applied the same tests of the candle, the charcoal and the iron wire. Extraordinary! He had obtained the same gas. Furthermore, there was no longer any doubt in his mind that the gas must have come from the atmosphere since he had heated the lead in the open air. It must be, he reasoned, an air completely free of phlogiston, and hence able to absorb an enormous amount of this element from anything burned in it.

It appeared to be an air, not only free of phlogiston, but possibly containing some hitherto unknown element, perhaps even one with rejuvenating life qualities. It would need much more investigating and testing, and here Joseph had a very definite problem—a financial one. Lord Shelburne had given him the sum of forty pounds a year for chemical apparatus. When Joseph had agreed to this rather strange contract with his Lordship, the sum had seemed adequate, but it gradually dawned on him that glass tubes bent to special shapes, retorts with curiously twisted necks, and bottles of odd sizes were not come by easily, and were constantly being broken. Furthermore, the glass makers seemed to raise their prices every time he appeared. He thought of asking for an increase in his allowance, but he couldn't because he was aware of a coolness between his patron and himself. He had noticed it for some time, and could trace it back to the sermon in which he had been free with criticism of the government. He could be mistaken, but the feeling was strong enough to prevent him from making any special request.

He mentioned his problem to the local chemist, who was sympathetic but in no position to offer any aid. Sometime later, however, when Mr. Josiah Wedgwood, who was official potter to the King, happened into his store, he said what a pity it was that so brilliant an experimenter as Dr. Priestley should be handicapped by the want of a few pounds. Mr. Wedgwood nodded agreement. Then he did something better than nod. He spoke to Sir George Savile who was a member of Parliament from Yorkshire and a very rich man. Sir George had known Joseph for some time, chiefly through a mutual belief in the Dissenters' creed and leniency toward the American colonies. Together, he and Mr. Wedgwood rounded up several of Joseph's friends, and made him an offer of an additional one hundred pounds a year to use for his experiments.

"I'm afraid," Joseph said when the offer was made, "that Lord Shelburne would be offended if I were to accept such a sum. He feels that he is doing quite well by me as it is." His friends understood, but they finally persuaded him to accept an additional forty pounds.

Joseph was about to purchase some new equipment to carry on his work with the new, mysterious air when Lord Shelburne announced that he was making a trip to the Continent and wanted him to go along. At some other time he would have been thrilled. Now he was anxious to follow up the investigation of his dephlogisticated air, as he had begun calling it. He shouldn't be leaving England. On the other hand, there was the question of his relations with Lord Shelburne which must not be further strained. Also, since he had recently been honored by the French Academy, and would doubtless be well received in Paris, he felt that he would be able to exchange ideas with French scientists. Also, he was doubtful about the purity of some of the chemicals supplied by his local chemist, and he knew that in Paris there was a chemist, a M. Cadet, who was famous for his reliability. Weighing these alternatives, he decided to offer no objections, and in September 1774 he and Lord Shelburne set out for the Continental trip.

Their journey took them across the channel to Belgium, Holland and Germany before retracing their steps to Paris. Very little in these countries impressed Joseph. The Belgians he considered careless in dress, and the Dutch especially uncouth in speech and actions. He wrote his wife frequently and in a letter to his pupil Henry he observed:

"Though you are not a man of gallantry, yet, as you are an observer of human nature, I must tell you what has struck me relating to the women we have seen. Many of them, even those who are well dressed, walk the streets in slippers without anything to cover the heel; so that with the exception of the toe, the whole foot is seen as they walk which, to me, who never saw the like before, looked slatternly and indelicate."

Another time he wrote:

"All the way we have come we were surprised at the prodigious quantity of tall, fine beans which are all standing, and with the plantations of tobacco and poppies. We could not imagine what use was made of so many poppy seeds, but we were informed that they get a great deal of oil from them, and that the many windmills we saw in that neighborhood were all employed to press that oil which is used for lamps."

France under Louis XVI was a curious place for two Englishmen to visit. She had only recently been defeated by England in the New World, and was showing marked sympathy with the discontented American colonists. But Lord Shelburne and Dr. Priestley were rather exceptional Englishmen. The Tory member of Parliament had hosts of influential friends at court and in society in general, and many gilded doors were opened to him. Joseph Priestley was not only a scientist of international repute and a member of the Academy, but his remarks and written statements about his sympathy with America had already reached France and had met with favor in many government circles. Although he was known as an extreme Protestant, toleration of all Protestants was the rule in France.

Joseph was anxious to visit Paris, but his companion was a little afraid that Joseph, with his flare for saying what he thought when he thought it, might disturb the tranquillity of the trip, which, had his Lordship cared to admit it, was being taken to get away from the rigors of Parliamentary debate.

"We are dining tonight," he said to Joseph, "with M. and Mme Lavoisier. He is, as you know, one of France's leading scientists and, although considerably younger than you, has had, I expect, a far more intensive training in the chemistry field. I trust you will forbear from any discussion that might prove in any way—er—embarrassing."

M. and Mme Lavoisier provided a most sumptuous dinner, quite in keeping with his standing as a member of the French nobility. The food and wine were excellent, and the guests represented some of the best scientific minds in France. There were M. Guyton de Morceau and M. Antoine François Fourcroy both of whom collaborated with M. Lavoisier in many of his experiments; there was M. Joseph Macquer, the oldest man present, famous for having helped make chemistry an independent science.

THE DISCOVERER OF OXYGEN

Others included M. Pierre Simon de la Place, M. Claude Berthollet and a M. John Hyacinth Magellan, a Portuguese scientist who belonged to perhaps more scientific societies than anyone present.

It was indeed a distinguished group, and Joseph was suitably impressed. He sat on Mme Lavoisier's left and did his best to become interested in her gay chatter. She was only seventeen and very pretty, and her conversation suited her age and looks. Joseph wondered how he could get out of the situation, when he was saved by M. Lavoisier.

"Dr. Priestley," he asked from the far end of the table, "what interesting experiment have you been making lately?"

The conversation had been quite general up to this time, but Lavoisier's question swept down the table like a sudden gust of wind, and turned every head toward Joseph. French was being spoken by everyone and he understood it quite well. However, when it came to speaking, he was not too sure of himself. A cautionary glance from Lord Shelburne on the other side of Mme Lavoisier didn't help to give him confidence. Hesitation, though, would be of no use, and he plunged in, speaking rather loudly to overcome any possible stammer. He told about his experiences with the red powder.

At the far end of the table M. Lavoisier was listening most attentively. His keen eyes, set in the thin, sensitive face, never for a moment left the stammering Yorkshireman.

"So I took a quantity of red lead and produced from it, with my burning glass, several containers of air," Joseph said. "I then tried the same tests I had used on Scheele's empyreal air with precisely the same results. So far I am unable to explain it, but one must admit that it is strange."

Strange indeed, and all the scientists began discussing it. All but Lavoisier. He sat in silent thought. He was just beginning to realize that he had been listening to a possible answer to a problem that had vexed him for months. Whenever he heated metals in a closed vessel and they calcined or turned to ashes, he found that about one fifth of the air disappeared. He supposed that it was because this air combined with the metal, but he was unable to recover it. When he heated the powder with carbon, the air simply combined with the carbon and produced fixed air. Now, from the mouth of this amateur, this Protestant minister, he was learning of a powder made from mercury, which, when heated, seemed to produce the very air he was unable to recover, the air that seemed to him to have simply disappeared.

Lavoisier was a great scientist, probably the greatest in France. He was also shrewd and thought by many to be not too scrupulous. He had great organizing ability, and did not hesitate to adopt as his own, any ideas conceived by other men, and organize them into a discovery. Joseph Priestley he recognized as an honest man. Any man, he reasoned, who would publicly disclose the secrets of his laboratory before having come to definite conclusions must be either honest or stupid, and Dr. Priestley certainly was not stupid. He had let Joseph talk on, quickly translating the Englishman's crude phraseology into proper chemical idiom, and storing it away in his mind.

97

After dinner, the men gathered in Lavoisier's library, and the talk turned to politics. Joseph found himself sitting next to M. Magellan, a chance encounter that started a long friendship. Magellan, although Portuguese, spoke English fluently, having settled in England in 1764, and it was a great relief to Joseph to be able to talk without effort. They discussed England, its progress in science and its problems in politics. Magellan was ten years older than Joseph, a tall, bulky man, towering almost six inches over him, but he was simple and unaffected in his manner and a Nonconformist in religion. The two had the same point of view on many subjects, and Joseph felt that here was a man whose acquaintance he must cultivate. Before the evening was over they had agreed to return to England together. Joseph had been getting restive and anxious to get back to his laboratory, and Magellan had to go back almost at once on business as corresponding secretary for the Royal Society. "Perhaps I can be of help to you," Magellan had said. "I happen to be corresponding secretary to the scientific societies in Paris, Madrid and St. Petersburg, as well as England, and I'll see to it that your experiments are known in all those places."

The next day M. Cadet, the best and most reliable chemist in Paris, had two rather special visitors. One was English and the other French. Here the difference ended. They each bought a small amount of the same chemical, a red powder of mercury, known in the trade as mercurius calcinatus per se. He served them both out of the same bottle and thought no more about it. He was a valuable link in a chain of events but, as Fate arranged it, he didn't know it.

Joseph had his precious supply of mercury powder; he had made an enthusiastic and valuable friend in Magellan; and he easily persuaded Lord Shelburne to continue his stay in Paris alone and let him get back to his laboratory.

Chapter Ten

Joseph reached England in January, 1775. His friend Magellan left him to go to his home in Islington with the promise to visit Yorkshire at the first opportunity. At home Mary, who was expecting their fourth child, was not at all well, and Joseph spent hours at her bedside. He told her all the details of his trip. "I left the French as I found them," he told her, "and whether they think better or worse of me on that account, I am very indifferent." Had he known what one Frenchman was thinking of him, he might have been less indifferent, but then he was not suspicious by nature. Sitting talking to Mary made him think of the weeks he had sat with his mother before she died. He waited on Mary constantly, and prayed morning and evening with her and the children. For a few weeks all thought of his new air was given up. He was the man of God reaching out to his maker for help.

In February his prayers were answered. His third son was born. His weeks of waiting were rewarded by Mary's quick return to health. At Lord Shelburne's request they named the boy Henry after his son who had become quite sickly and was not expected to live very much longer.

Joseph was soon back at work looking for the answer to the riddle of his new air. He found the mercurius calcinatus per se which he had purchased from M. Cadet in Paris eminently satisfactory, and he filled a dozen bottles with the air. He had already had dramatic proof of its power to support a burning flame. He had suspected for some time that his new air was even purer than common air, and the best way to find out was by his nitrous air. This was colorless, insoluble in water, and had the curious quality, when mixed with ordinary air in the proportion of one volume to two volumes, of reducing the whole mixture to one and eight-tenths volumes. This experiment had amazed him. "It was," he often said, "as though a quantity of air devoured another quantity of air as large as itself, and yet is so far from gaining any addition to its bulk that it is considerably diminished by it." If mixed with wholly bad or noxious air there was, he found, no reduction in volume. A far better test, Joseph decided, than sacrificing a live mouse.

Taking one of the bottles of the precious air, he carefully measured two volumes of it and one volume of nitrous air, and led them into a jar over water. He watched the water rise and measured the resulting volume. He was astonished with what he found. Instead of the three volumes he started with, he now had one and six tenths, even less than in the case of ordinary air or atmosphere. There was certainly no doubt about it. His new air was the purest he had yet found. Thoroughly dephlogisticated, he said to himself.

Combustion or the burning flame had been improved by it, but what about respiration? He must try it. He had several mice in his cage. He looked at them and smiled to himself. These little animals were about to solve a problem for him—perhaps a solution that would affect the whole world. Joseph took two identical glass vessels, filled one with dephlogisticated air and the other with a like amount of ordinary air, and inverted them over water. He had arranged a small floating platform with raised edges in each jar. He carefully passed the two mice up through the water onto the platforms. They wriggled at first and finally quieted down on their precarious perches.

Joseph had no idea how long he would have to wait. He pulled up a chair, took his flute, at which he had become fairly proficient since his lessons from Mr. Eddowes, and began playing softly. He kept his eyes fixed on the little victims, watching for any sign that might provide an answer. He had carefully checked his clock. Five minutes passed. Then ten. He stopped playing and, with his eyes still fixed on the cages, laid his flute gently on the floor. The mouse in the jar of dephlogisticated air seemed quite normal, its nose quivering as it breathed, its body occasionally and quite naturally changing position. In the other jar the mouse seemed to be breathing in gasps, its eyes almost completely closed, and in fifteen minutes it was lying quite still. Joseph reached in and carefully drew the little body out of its prison. He warmed it in his hands, but it was dead.

The other mouse seemed quite happy, but at the end of twenty minutes Joseph noticed that its movements were becoming a little sluggish. Five minutes later its breathing became very irregular and its eyes began closing. He left it another five minutes and then carefully removed it, cold and wet. Taking it to the fire he held it near the coals. He could feel its little heart beating and the sensation made his own beat faster. In a few minutes the tiny eyes opened and the body began to squirm. Joseph put it back in its dry cage and sat down to recover his own breath. There was no doubt in his mind. This air, whatever it might be, was capable of supporting respiration, as well as combustion, better than ordinary air. It was not only a vindication of his nitrous air test, but a proof that this air was, as he had thought, either thoroughly dephlogisticated, or filled with some life-giving element. Or, he reasoned, it could be that ordinary air contained some element that poisoned life. Either way, it was the opening of a new chapter in his study of air.

That night Joseph slept peacefully. His weeks of watching over Mary had wearied him, and this latest experiment had been accompanied by nervous tension. But there was also a delicious feeling of satisfaction that calmed his nerves the moment he lay down. He was up early and spent the day repeating his experiment. When he kept getting the same results after four or five times, he varied the situation. He noted that the vessel in which his first mouse had lived still contained some of the new air. He put another mouse in without changing the air, and to his astonishment thirty minutes went by before the little animal became unconscious. The vessel had been in a cold place and he had neglected to warm it so, unhappily, the mouse died of cold but not, Joseph noted gleefully, for want of some life-giving air.

Then an idea occurred to him. He was convinced beyond doubt that the dephlogisticated air had kept the mice alive. He was prepared to report this to the Royal Society, but mice were very small. His findings might be true for such little forms of life, but what about human beings? He decided to experiment on himself. He could hardly put himself in the position of the mice, but if he were to inhale some of the air he might find an answer. It was dangerous, but to Joseph that was unimportant when something was to be learned from an experiment. In case anything unfortunate should happen, he wrote his friend Magellan, asking him to come and help with an experiment. True to his earlier promise, Magellan dropped everything and came. Joseph made up a fresh supply of the dephlogisticated air and, smiling a little grimly at Magellan, inserted one end of a glass tube in the container, put the other end in his mouth and inhaled deeply. As he took the tube out of his mouth, Magellan looked at him questioningly.

"Well?" he asked.

Joseph shrugged his shoulders. "You try it," he said, handing the glass tube to Magellan who took a long draught of the air.

"I don't notice that it is any different from common air," Magellan commented as he put the tube down and closed the glass vessel. But Joseph had a questioning look. "Wait just a moment or two," he said. "I thought that too, at first, but now my breath and my whole chest seem peculiarly light and easy." The two men stood silent for a while. Then Magellan nodded agreement. "I see what you mean. What do you make of it?"

"The first thing that occurs to me," Joseph replied, "is that, whatever it is, it should be a great help in lung cases that are particularly morbid. Perhaps this air is better able to carry off the phlogiston that is putrefying." He paused and there was a faint smile around his mouth as he continued. "There seems to be just one possible danger. The candle flame burned brighter, but burned out faster in this air. Perhaps if we breathe it continuously we might burn out more quickly—even if we were more brilliant."

Magellan laughed. "Can't you forget that you are a minister and therefore a moralist?" he asked. "Who's going to live solely on dephlogisticated air?"

"Perhaps you're right," Joseph agreed. "I shall leave that to the doctors." As he spoke he was already on the track of a new use for his air. His hands were filling a small bladder with it from one of his bottles. He inserted a glass tube in the mouth of the bladder, and by compressing this he puffed the air on a smoldering piece of wood. It instantly burst into flame.

"We ought to attach a large balloon to this," he suggested, "and supply it from a reservoir of this air. There is no telling what it would do."

"Now, you *are* dreaming," replied Magellan, laughing. Unfortunately he had no crystal ball.

Joseph tried various other substances such as quick lime and spirits of niter. On March 15, 1775, he wrote a long letter to Sir John Pringle, president of the Royal Society of London. He described in great detail what he had done, pointed out that it was his conviction that the basis of our atmosphere was niter, and that there was no doubt but that this new air was the life-giving element of the atmosphere—a completely dephlogisticated air.

On April 30, 1775, a little over a month after Joseph had reported to the Royal Society in London, Antoine Lavoisier presented a paper to the French Academy describing how he had discovered a life-giving air which made up a small percentage of the atmosphere. He called it *oxygène*, a name derived from the Greek word *oxys*, meaning sharp, and *gen*, to be born. Being a member of the French Academy, Joseph received this particular bulletin in due course. He read it carefully a second time. One part in particular astonished him. The Frenchman, after enumerating the many difficulties he had encountered with various calxes that could only be reduced by the addition of charcoal, wrote, "I then decided to study another kind of calx which would have the property of being reducible without the addition of charcoal, and I decided that mercurius calcinatus per se was eminently suitable, and it is with that that I have had success."

There was no doubt about it. He had given Lavoisier the hint that had made him, in his own words, "decide to try mercurius calcinatus per se—" This *oxygène* was nothing more than his own dephlogisticated air.

Chapter Eleven

The suspicions aroused by Lavoisier's report to the French Academy were difficult for Joseph to believe. There was some murmuring among certain members of both societies, but the two reports were simply accepted without any public statement of priority. Joseph himself was inherently honest, and the remarks he had made at the French scientist's dinner table had, he supposed, been accepted as strictly confidential. The majority of French men of science, he had concluded after his trip, were definitely opposed to Protestantism but it never occurred to him that they were dishonest. Lavoisier called the air *oxygène*, but that was because he did not go along, as Joseph did, with the currently accepted theory of phlogiston. The name didn't really matter, Joseph thought. It was his dephlogisticated air, whatever other odd names might be conjured up for it.

Unfortunately Benjamin Franklin had left England only a month before or Joseph would have sought advice from his old friend. As it was, he received a letter from him in June of 1775 that for the moment put aside all considerations of chemistry, and took him into one of his other worlds, that of politics. It appeared, Franklin wrote, that the American colonies were on the verge of revolution. All America was exasperated by the warlike attitude of the English prime minister, Lord North, who had doubled the fortifications at Boston. In the next few weeks anything could happen.

So, Joseph mused, no sensible advice had been taken by the government—neither that of Franklin, nor Burke, nor Chatham, nor the city of London itself, which had petitioned the King for tolerance toward the colonies. He thought of all the words he himself had written since 1769 urging Christian forbearance in this political strife. He spoke to Lord Shelburne about it.

"As I told you, Joseph," Shelburne said, shrugging his shoulders, "the King is stubborn and Lord North is his tool. We will simply have to accept the situation, and hope for the best." Then he added quietly but with the force of an order, "I think under the circumstances it would be unwise for you to meddle much more in politics."

This, to Joseph, was almost like saying that a minister should not meddle in religion, so much had he identified all his activities with his God. He couldn't, however, oppose Lord Shelburne to his face. After all, he had Mary and the children to consider, not to mention his laboratory and his precious experiments. He was faced with a dilemma, and he wished that his friend Franklin had not returned to America. A letter and a reply took three months, so he would have to act as he thought best, without outside advice. After talking it over with Mary, at her suggestion he decided not to write any more political pamphlets for a while. He would, he told her, continue expressing himself to Franklin and Burke. Of course, if they chose to quote him publicly there would be nothing he could do to stop it.

In July war definitely broke out between England and her colonies, and anything Joseph might have written or said in an attempt to prevent it was now useless. He filled his time in his laboratory, writing frequent reports to the Royal Society and producing two more volumes on air.

His first success in science had really been in the field of electricity, and during the next few years he experimented with a combination of air or gas and electric discharges. His general method was to confine a particular gas over water or mercury and send an electric spark through it, carefully observing any change in nature or volume. One day, quite by chance, he decided to put some foreign matter into the water. Part of the excitement of all his experiments came from putting together substances quite unrelated, and watching for the least significant change. He had often seen his father, when dyeing cloth, use a dye from a funguslike lichen plant. It was called litmus from the old Norman name for lichen. Joseph dyed some water over which he had confined ordinary atmospheric air, and passed a spark through it repeatedly. Two strange, though unconnected, things happened—the volume of the air in the vessel decreased considerably, and the water, colored blue by the litmus, turned red.

Then he decided to try another kind of air, and he substituted ammonia gas which he had confined over mercury. To his surprise, when he passed a spark through it, the volume of the air increased instead of decreasing as had the ordinary air. It was evident that this caustic alkaline gas had undergone some very basic chemical change. It had, he found, no effect on common air, nor was it affected in any way by his nitrous air test. Furthermore, it was highly inflammable. It was undoubtedly the inflammable air of the ancients.

Joseph wrote out all these experiments with the greatest detail, and reported them to the Royal Society which published them in its *Philosophical Transactions*. He also prepared them in book form under the title *Observations and Experiments on Air*. By 1779 he had three volumes completed, and much material for a fourth.

Meanwhile the war in the colonies continued. France had just made a formal treaty of assistance, and the British government was ready to change prime ministers at any moment. Joseph corresponded constantly with Edmund Burke and Ben Franklin, expressing his joy in the successes of the "seekers after liberty" as he called them. He even so far forgot his resolution as to make references in his sermons when invited to preach at the local chapel.

He produced a fiery pamphlet—*Letters to a Philosophical Unbeliever*—in which he offered proof of a God and Providence to any and all doubters. This was violently objected to by a man who signed himself "Hammon" and who, to Joseph's surprise, turned out to be none other than Dr. Matthew Turner whose chemistry lectures at Warrington had so intrigued him. He then proposed writing a rather violent pamphlet to be entitled *Disquisitions on Matter and Spirit*, but his friend Magellan read it and urged him not to go ahead. It would, he pointed out, injure his Lordship's standing in the government to be in any way associated with concepts that might be contrary to the tenets of the Established Church.

THE DISCOVERER OF OXYGEN

"There comes a time, Magellan," Joseph replied, "when, if one is engaged in the cause of an important truth, certain persons must be hurt."

"You're taking a great risk," his friend warned him.

"It is one that I am quite willing to take," Joseph retorted. "I feel that my success in philosophical studies gives me a certain prestige in advancing so fundamental a thing as Christianity."

This was all very well in theory, but when, a few weeks later, Lord Shelburne opened his paper one morning and read that his "literary companion," Joseph Priestley, was considered publicly to be an unbeliever in revelation and an avowed atheist, the matter took an extremely practical turn. Lord Shelburne's attitude toward Joseph became definitely cool.

Late in 1779 Joseph wrote to Franklin telling him of the strain in relations between him and his patron, and asked if he didn't think that a termination of the contract should be made. Franklin, being diplomatically inclined, did not wish to become involved in personal matters, especially with so important a person as Lord Shelburne, so he advised Joseph to put off any change until the end of the current year when a natural change could be made.

So Joseph decided to wait. The following June would mark the eighth year of his employment, and as it had been on a year to year basis, that seemed to him the best time to make the break. In the meantime he continued experimenting in his laboratory and carrying on his duties at the castle. The last few months were not particularly happy. Joseph was frequently called upon to perform electric experiments for his Lordship's guests, who, Joseph knew, had no real interest in or curiosity about the strange actions of electricity. They wanted to be amused, and promptly went home and forgot all about it. It gave Joseph a mischievous but real satisfaction when some particularly objectionable guest was persuaded to receive an electric shock, the climax of all his demonstrations, to make sure that the charge of electricity was unusually strong. All in all, Joseph began counting the days that were left of his association with Lord Shelburne.

June 1780 finally came around. Joseph and his patron were having one of their usual talks in the library. Joseph was waiting for an opportunity to tender his resignation when Lord Shelburne gave him a perfect opening.

"How would you like to go to Ireland?" he asked rather abruptly, and continued without waiting for an answer. "I have, as you probably know, extensive holdings there, and as I shall be very busy here with the war and all, I should like someone like yourself over there to keep an eye on things."

Joseph knew perfectly well that this was a circuitous way of saying that he was no longer wanted at Bowood. He was rather flattered that Shelburne had used this method to avoid hurting his feelings. It implied that there was still a not too unfriendly feeling in the air. Joseph also knew that the critical situation with the American colonies threatened the fall of the existing ministry of Lord North, and that Shelburne was mentioned in several quarters as being a possible successor. Naturally, Joseph's thinking continued, a man like me would not be popular as a political playmate for someone aspiring to regain the favor of the King and become prime minister.

As for Ireland, he had heard a lot about it from his Lordship as well as from Edmund Burke who was born there, and he had always thought he would like to go. It would be easy living for his family who had done nothing but struggle ever since leaving Warrington. On the other hand, by accepting the offer he would be placing himself under obligation to Lord Shelburne, and he had grown tired of that over the last eight years. He was being shelved, and that was something that Joseph at forty-seven resented.

"My Lord," he said finally and very firmly, "your offer of this holding in Ireland is very generous, but I should prefer to remain in England. My wife and children love it and I love it, and my friends are here. I think, therefore, that I must refuse it and, if I may, accept your original offer of a yearly stipend of a hundred and fifty pounds if that is still your intention."

Lord Shelburne knew Joseph well enough to know that when his mind was made up there was no changing it, and so Joseph joined his wife and children in their home in Calne, his precious laboratory equipment piled high in one room until future plans could be made.

Chapter Twelve

Unable for the moment to carry on any experiments, Joseph passed the time happily with his children. Sarah was a lovely girl of seventeen, Joseph and William, aged twelve and nine, were still just little wild Indians, and Henry was a rather delicate baby of three.

Fieldhead, Daventry, Needham, Nantwich, Warrington, Leeds and Calne. Seven different homes in forty-seven years; and now he must decide on an eighth. He had promised Mary when they left Warrington that Leeds would be their final home; he was glad to be there as a clergyman, and in spite of his promise to Mary, he didn't really regret his eight years with Lord Shelburne. He had accomplished more in his laboratory than he had during all the years before. He was sorry that his leaving was marred by any ill feeling, but it was not in his nature to pretend, even when it meant his livelihood. He thought things and he said things. He was not a politician as was Lord Shelburne, living a life balanced between truth and political convenience. He had spoken his mind ever since he had defied the Reverend Amos Woburn at fifteen, and he fully intended to go on speaking it whatever the consequences. He often told Mary that his favorite passage in the Bible was the twentieth verse of the fourteenth chapter of St. Paul's Epistle to the Corinthians—"Prove all things; hold fast to that which is good." This allowed of no compromise.

On this June day in 1780, Joseph sat gazing at the room piled high with chemical equipment, chairs and tables. He was faced with a situation to which no particular passage in scripture seemed to apply. He was out of a job, his income was cut exactly in half, and he had a wife and four children to support. The same group of friends, headed by Josiah Wedgwood, who had helped defray his laboratory expenses while he was at Lord Shelburne's, again offered to help him in his present dilemma. Joseph was hesitant about accepting more financial aid from these kind friends, especially since he had twice been offered a government pension through the influence of Lord Shelburne. If he had accepted this, he thought to himself, he would have been beholden to the whims of the government and would not have been able to express opinions of his own. He couldn't honorably criticize any group that was keeping him alive, and he knew perfectly well that he couldn't agree with everything they did. His friends on the other hand believed in him, and his only obligation would be to continue his fight for truth in his three worlds of religion, science and politics. So he decided to accept help from them.

With the financial problem out of the way, Joseph had to decide where his new home should be and what he would do. Mary solved the first question through one of her brothers, John Wilkinson, who had an iron foundry in the city of Birmingham, in central England, and was prosperous and influential. He urged his sister and her family to move there. Joseph agreed as he had a feeling that his children would grow up in a better atmosphere among friends and relations than among strangers. Joseph, of course, knew of Birmingham and it brought back memories of his father. As a weaver, Jonas Priestley had occasion to use a great many pins, and Joseph as a child had always been warned not to play with them as they came all the way from Birmingham, were hard to get and were very expensive. He inquired and found that the religion of the people of Birmingham, while largely Church of England, was also considered the most liberal in all of England, the town having a new, large Dissenting congregation. In his heart, Joseph wanted to get back to active church work, and with this picture in view both the last problems appeared solved, and so he packed up and made his eighth move, this time to Warwickshire.

Birmingham on the river Rea, the ancient seat of the Lords of Birmingham, had been a market town or trading center since the thirteenth century, and in the eighteenth century was a busy manufacturing town, producing such things as pins, anvils, augurs, bags, bedscrews, boxes, buttons and toys. Prince Rupert, a nephew of Charles I, had partly destroyed it during the civil wars in 1643, and twenty years later it was swept by the plague which ravaged England. Since then it had grown to its present importance in the economy of England.

Joseph settled with his family in a rented house on the outskirts of the town in a pleasant area known as Fairhill, and set up his laboratory for the third time. While he had always had his children much on his mind, he left the details to Mary. Their schooling was taken care of in the classes connected with the new Dissenters' Chapel. Young

Joseph had always displayed great interest in his father's chemical experiments, which pleased Joseph, and John Wilkinson had promised that when he was older William could be taken on at the foundry as an apprentice. As for Henry, the youngest, Joseph secretly hoped that he would become a minister.

There were kindred spirits in the town, many of whom he had known personally or by repute. There was James Watt, who had recently perfected a pump for drawing water from flooded mines, and his partner in the steam engine business, Matthew Boulton; Josiah Wedgwood, who had consistently aided Joseph and who kept him supplied with retorts and bottles from his pottery works, was a very frequent visitor, and through him he met William Herschel, a well-known astronomer though not yet patronized by royalty, and John Smeaton, who designed the Eddystone Lighthouse off the coast of Cornwall.

All these men met regularly at each other's homes, calling their group the Lunar Society because they arranged their meetings to coincide with the full of the moon, the streets at other times being dark and dangerous.

Their talks covered every field and were quite informal, the sort of discussions Joseph liked, and he was able to talk very freely about any matter since opinions were not barred because of religious or political prejudice. Each man in turn was expected to present a subject for discussion. Shortly after joining the Lunar Society, Joseph brought up his favorite subject of dephlogisticated air.

James Watt, the engineer, was in an argumentative

mood. "I understand," he said, "that M. Lavoisier in France calls this air oxygen."

"That," Priestley answered with confidence, "is because he claims there is no such thing as phlogiston."

"How else can a metal be converted into a powder?" Watt asked.

"Exactly," Joseph agreed. "In the heating process the phlogiston is taken out of it. Lavoisier claims that it is the addition of air generated by the heat that causes the metal to disintegrate."

"But as I understand M. Lavoisier," Watt persisted, "there is a distinct gain in weight of the calx or powder over the metal."

Appearing not to hear this point, Joseph observed, "That mercury in its metallic state does contain phlogiston, or inflammable air, is evident from the production of nitrous air by the solution of it in spirits of niter. I make nitrous air from nothing, I repeat—from nothing but nitrous vapor and inflammable air; so that it indisputably consists of these two ingredients."

Watt stubbornly went back to his question. "But how do you account for the increase in weight that M. Lavoisier found by, I believe, weighing the rust from a piece of iron?"

"I have to admit," Joseph answered, "that there is a definite gain in weight, but though M. Lavoisier's explanation is ingenious, I feel that the proper explanation is that phlogiston has a quality of levitation—notice that a candle flame burns up—and so, of course, as you remove phlogiston from the metal, you naturally reduce its power of levitation and it becomes heavier."

Joseph believed in this firmly, and he also thought, though he didn't say it publicly, that Lavoisier used the name oxygen merely to cover the fact that he had appropriated Joseph's new air for his own use.

After a few weeks of discussion the group was convinced, and Boulton wrote to Josiah Wedgwood, "We have long talked of phlogiston without knowing what we talked about; but now that Dr. P. hath brought the matter to light we can pour that element out of one vessel into another; can tell how much of it by accurate measurement is necessary to reduce a calx to a metal, which is easily done, and without putting that calx into contact with any visible thing. In short, the goddess of levity can be measured and weighed like other matter. For the rest I refer you to the doctor himself."

Being a friend of many of the influential men in Birmingham, and bringing with him as he did an international reputation as a scientist, it wasn't long before Joseph was sought out by others. There were in the city two large Dissenters' chapels, the Old and the New meetinghouses, and a few months after his arrival he received an invitation to assist at the New Meetinghouse. Joseph was delighted, as he wanted to get back to serious theological duties. He accepted, with the stipulation that his activities would be limited to weekend preaching and catechizing. He wanted time for his chemical work and also for a writing project that he had been planning for some time.

This project was ambitious and fraught with definite

danger for the writer, as it would attack many of the rituals and beliefs of the Established Church of England. He had hesitated to produce it while living with Lord Shelburne for obvious reasons, but now that he was free of him, and living in a city with a very large Dissenting population, he decided to go ahead with it. There were, of course, Church of England congregations in Birmingham, though no Roman Catholic. They were large and powerful, and they tolerated the Dissenters merely because legally they could do nothing about it. By a curious quirk of the law, Dissenters could not be prosecuted in Birmingham for the reason that it was not a corporate town but what was known as a manor. This, Joseph felt, would permit him safely to write what he pleased on religious subjects, no matter whose toes he might tread on. This was wishful thinking, but since he did not know it at the time, Joseph went boldly ahead.

His book was to have the challenging title of *History of the Corruptions of Christianity*, and was to be an attack on the errors and superstitions which had grown up around the simplicity of the early Gospels. What he wanted to do was to get at the mind—the very thoughts—of the common Christian people in the first age, and to make their primary understanding of the Scriptures the basis for true, modern interpretation.

His congregation at the New Meetinghouse had agreed unanimously to all his terms and had, besides, raised the sum of two hundred pounds to help him in the publication of theological writing. They were loyal, but they underestimated the radical nature of Joseph Priestley's thoughts.

He had a quiet and persuasive pulpit manner, which he had developed largely to overcome his tendencies toward stammering, but the written word was something different.

The book appeared in two volumes in 1782 and caused a sensation. Such sentences as "Bishops are recorded in all histories as the most jealous, the most timorous and, of course, the most vindictive of men" didn't exactly militate in Joseph's favor. His congregation read the two volumes and privately agreed with him, but since it was more radical than they had expected, they kept quiet. Not so the members of the Established Church. The *Monthly Review*, a much-read Birmingham paper, attacked Joseph in most violent terms. The writer of the article was a Mr. Badcock, a former Dissenter but now a member of the Established Church. Joseph was surprised and a little hurt since Mr. Badcock had been a great friend of his at Leeds. It was impossible for Joseph to believe that true friendship could be wrecked on any point of contention.

Nevertheless, Mr. Badcock was violent and unrelenting. "In the name of modesty, Dr. Priestley," he wrote, "do not write as if it was a matter settled by universal suffrage that all the good sense in the world, all intellectual freedom, and all truth were confined to you." To which scathing comment a minister friend of Joseph's replied, "Mr. Badcock, Dr. Priestley will be found to have kindled the greatest light that ever illumined the Age of George III. The darkness of your little mind comprehendeth it not."

The fight was on. A month later, the coffeehouses in Birmingham buzzed with news that copies of *Corrup-*

tions of Christianity which had reached Holland had been summarily burned by the public hangman in the square at Dadrecht. The effect of this expression of public opinion on Joseph might have been disastrous, but it so happened that at almost the same time that he received the news from Dadrecht, he had a letter from his friend Magellan in Paris. Lavoisier, it seemed, after eight years had at last admitted that Joseph was the discoverer of the air he called oxygen. In his letter, Magellan quoted Lavoisier whom he had heard at a talk on oxygen at the French Academy, "—this air which Mr. Priestley discovered about the same time as myself, and even, I believe, before me—"

The use of the word "mister" instead of "doctor" slightly irritated Joseph, but the important thing was that he was vindicated publicly in the matter of dephlogisticated air. It followed, Joseph assured himself, that his vindication in the matter of religious corruption was only a matter of waiting long enough, and he completely ignored the growing criticism.

He ignored the pieces in the newspaper. He ignored the talk he overheard at coffeehouses. He ignored what he was told pople were saying. It was criticism of his ideas. He still had his Dissenting friends and his fellow members of the Lunar Society and, as a matter of fact, many Church of England members who were not afraid of the charges against their doctrines.

One day a very small incident occurred that Joseph found rather more difficult to ignore. Mary told him that she had been refused bread at the baker's shop where they traded and had had to walk a long way to another one.

Joseph felt that it was very petty of anyone to incon-
venience his wife, who was not overly strong, just because
of a difference in religious opinions. He went to see the
baker, John Green, and pointed out that his money was
as good as the next man's, that what he had said in the book
was only the truth as he saw it and had nothing to do with
bread. After half an hour with Mr. Green, Joseph realized
that it was very doubtful that the man had even read the
book, and therefore arguing with him was quite futile. He
took his trade elsewhere and decided to ignore Mr. Green
as he had everyone else. What was hard for him to ignore
was the realization of the gross ignorance on which much
of the criticism was built.

Chapter Thirteen

Joseph Priestley continued to ignore the fight as far as personal invective went. Of the critics he often said to his friends, "I am thankful that it gives less disturbance to me than to themselves." He continued writing religious truth as he saw it, producing a *History of Early Christian Opinions Regarding Jesus Christ* in four volumes as an answer to some criticisms of his *Corruptions of Christianity*, and an annual pamphlet in defense of Unitarian doctrines.

His fame as a scientist, his skill in the pulpit, and his radical views on religion and politics made it inevitable that he should become a central figure in the life of Birmingham. People took sides. Priestley became a conversational "must" in all coffeehouses. The intellectual members of the Established Church disliked him for dogmatically sound reasons, and they were supported unthinkingly but with loud enthusiasm by the ignorant members of the Establishment such as John Green, the baker, and his friends. Once interest was aroused in Joseph Priestley, his past became of necessity an open book. His criticism of the government, dating back fifteen years, his support of the revolted American colonies, and even the fact that he had not been very popular at Needham, became subjects for popular discussion.

Joseph, however, carried on. In a quiet way he even added fuel to the fire by establishing a Sunday school class.

This was objected to as tending to corrupt the youth of Birmingham, who should, so the critics claimed, be brought up to respect the laws of England and the tenets of the Established Church. Joseph merely smiled and established three more classes. These were well attended, and he persuaded the church authorities for the convenience of his students to add a library of religious books including all of his own, which made a considerable number. In the eyes of the orthodox this was another count against Priestley.

According to his agreement with the members of the New Meetinghouse, the days between Sundays were spent in his laboratory or with his family. He made frequent trips to London, kept up a steady correspondence with all his friends, and attended regularly the meetings of the Lunar Society which, possibly through the fact of his membership, had become known as the Lunatic Society.

One evening at a meeting of this group, he got into a discussion of the possible conversion of air into water or vice versa. There were various opinions pro and con, and Joseph decided to carry on some experiments. The following day he set up his apparatus. On a piece of broken earthenware crucible which could yield no air, he put a small quantity of minium or red lead out of which all air had been extracted. He then placed it on a convenient stand and introduced it into a large receiver filled with inflammable air confined over water. By means of his burning lens he completely dried the minium and watched very carefully. The minium became black and then ran in the form of a perfect lead. At the same time he noticed that the air diminished at a great rate and the water ascended in the receiver. Two questions came to mind. Was the air actually decomposing or was it being absorbed by the water? Joseph felt that the former was probably true. The calx was actually imbibing something from the air. If there were such a thing as phlogiston which he firmly believed, the inflammable air, he imagined, must consist of it and something else, possibly dephlogisticated air or even water. The only thing he could be sure of in this was that the water was increasing as the air diminished, but this was hardly conversion since the calx was imbibing at least some of the air.

The next day he tried another approach. He put a mixture of inflammable air and common air in a thick glass container and sent an electric spark through it. This heating of a substance with an electric spark which Joseph had been doing for some time was always an exciting method. The reaction was quicker than in the case of fire or a burning lens. It required only a fraction of a second for some new marvel to unfold, some hitherto hidden secret of God's creation to be exposed to the eye of man. There was a crackle—and almost instantly a dew was formed on the inside of the container. Though it had the appearance of water and seemed closer to actual conversion of air into water, Joseph was not wholly convinced.

Nevertheless, he communicated his experiment to Henry Cavendish in London. He had checked with him on his early experiment which established the measurement of electric energy, and he had great respect for the opinion of this wealthy recluse whose work was always not only

original but extremely accurate. As Joseph had expected
he had an immediate reply.

> For years I have been trying to determine the composi-
> tion of water. Now, you have given me a most valuable
> hint by your recent experiment in which you exploded
> common air and inflammable air, and found a residue of
> dew on the container. If this dew is water, it should be
> determinable by measurement how much of each air is
> in it, and whether or not there is anything left over. I shall
> keep you informed.
>
> Your friend
>
> H. Cavendish

Soon after, true to his word, Cavendish wrote to Joseph
and reported that after years of effort he had at last determined the components of water. He had, he said, put carefully measured amounts of the two airs, common and
inflammable, in a vessel as Priestley had done. When a
spark was sent through the mixture all the hydrogen, as
inflammable air was beginning to be called, and about one
fifth of the common air lost its elasticity and condensed
into a dew which lined the glass. This four fifths of the
common air that was left was noxious; a mouse died in it
and a candle was extinguished. Water was undoubtedly
made up of two parts of hydrogen and one part of oxygen,
or Priestley's dephlogisticated air, which he himself had
shown was one fifth of common air.

Joseph read the letter. How close he himself had come
to determining the composition of water! The same dew
had appeared on his glass vessel, and the proportions must

have been the same, but he had not detected it. Cavendish had followed his procedure, but with greater care and accuracy. Joseph wrote at once congratulating his friend. It was not in his nature to be jealous. Even when he recently heard that Lavoisier had announced the use of dephlogisticated air blown on a charcoal fire to increase the intensity of the flame, he had kept silent, although in his own mind he was thinking back to the time when he blew his air from a bladder and suggested to Magellan the use of a huge bellows. He refused to get into petty squabbles. If the truth were found, what matter who found it?

In 1787 Joseph had a letter from Magellan who was in France reporting to the French Academy. There was brewing, Magellan told him, a serious threat of revolution. France was tottering on the brink of bankruptcy. M. Calonne, the comptroller of the currency, had called a large group of rich notables to Versailles and had asked them to help by submitting to a new form of taxation which would include them as well as the small shopkeepers and peasants. The notables had refused, and word of this refusal had spread until it was talked about in all the communities, all the farms, all the shops. The little people of France heard it and it stirred old-time jealousy into hatred.

To Joseph this was an echo of the plaint of the American colonists in 1775. To him this wasn't just another revolution—a mere political squabble. He saw the peasants and poorer classes of France as human beings denied the right to a full life by the selfishness and greed of a ruling class. It was the way he viewed all injustice—a violation of one of the fundamental laws of God's world. He girded himself for another campaign for liberty. He began a correspondence with many of his scientific friends in Paris, and talked about the situation freely in Birmingham. He wrote to his friend Burke and, to his surprise, received a rather cool letter, expressing no great sympathy with the revolutionists of France.

Joseph was puzzled. He remembered so well his first meeting with Edmund Burke when the question of political liberty had been brought up. There followed Burke's fight for the cause of the American colonies. Joseph could not understand why this new fight for liberty did not enthuse his friend as much as it did him. Burke had always been devoted to the Dissenters' group in their struggle for religious liberty, and his new attitude seemed to be almost the desertion of a cause.

Then in 1789 the Bastille, the former citadel and dreary prison for political prisoners in Paris, fell to a mob hungry for freedom. To Joseph and his friends, this was a symbol of the triumph of liberty. He looked again to Burke for support and again was disappointed. Following the fall of the Bastille, Burke published a bitter tirade against the whole revolution in France, *Reflections on the French Revolution*. Joseph read it and his fighting spirit was aroused. It even occurred to him that Edmund Burke was being paid by the King to attack anything that was in any way anti-Royalist. It was the only explanation he could think of for such a sudden and complete change in Burke's thinking. He wrote a powerful answer, not mincing matters because of former friendship. "Your imagination is heated and your ideas confused," he wrote, and reminded

129

Burke of his violent support of the American Revolution. He hoped to persuade him. He disliked losing a friend, but the break seemed inevitable. It was a case of two strong and stubborn men on opposite sides of a cause.

Joseph would have turned to Ben Franklin but he died the year following the fall of the Bastille, so he fought on all alone. It took time from his laboratory; it held up publication of his last volume of *Observations and Experiments* and, as if this were not enough, a new Parliamentary attack was made on him and his Dissenting followers. An act was being debated in Parliament known as the "Corporation and Test Act," the sole purpose of which was to strengthen the Established Church at the expense of all Dissenters. It proposed to deny employment to any but Church of England men, and would require a religious test for any government position. To Joseph's dismay, Edmund Burke was one of its keenest supporters. The break with his friend was indeed wide.

The years immediately following the fall of the Bastille were hectic and complicated for Joseph. His brother-in-law John Wilkinson had never agreed with him in religious or political matters. When the Parliamentary attacks became common knowledge, he refused to continue to employ William in his foundry. Although this was a blow to Joseph, it was some consolation to have William once more at home since Sarah, his daughter, had just been married to a Mr. William Finch and was living at Heath Forge, some distance from Birmingham.

Joseph's health suffered and for months he lived on a diet of vegetables, finding himself unable to take the long walks

through the countryside he had enjoyed since his childhood. He wrote and preached. There were two battles for
justice, and he waded into the middle of each, sparing no
one, least of all himself. He carried his arguments into his
sermons and discussed them after church. He advocated
calm, patient persuasion in the matter of injustice toward
Dissenters but, he said in one sermon, "While we join in
asserting our own rights, let us not be unmindful of the
rights of others, especially the rights of humanity of which
the poor Negroes have long been deprived, and also of the
just claim of all men to the right of a free and equal government. Let us, with our prayers and good wishes at least,
aid a neighboring nation and all who are now struggling
for liberty, civil and religious, throughout the world; that
the voice of the oppressor may everywhere cease to be
heard; that by this means we may see the nearer approach
of those glorious and happy times when wars shall cease
to the ends of the earth, and when the kingdoms of this
world shall become the kingdoms of God and of his
Christ."

The Dissenting congregations in Birmingham agreed
with him wholeheartedly. As a matter of fact their numbers increased, but Joseph became more and more a target
for abuse from those who disagreed with him politically or
in religious matters. He had always felt that his scientific
work placed him in a position from which he could ignore
all this, but he soon began to wonder. His pamphlets in
defense of his beliefs were carefully worded and scien-
tifically organized. He kept out of them any rancor he
might feel. He wrote thirteen letters to Burke, pleading

with him as supposedly a friend of liberty not to oppose the Dissenters by upholding the Test Act.

"The Church of Christ," he wrote, "is built upon a rock—and the gates of Hell shall not prevail against it. I have resided here in Birmingham only ten years, and there are now being built the eighth, ninth and tenth places of worship for us, and not a single new Church of England building. We desire no advantage from the Established Church. Why, then, ought we suffer any disadvantage by nonconformity to it?"

Joseph was nearing the age of sixty, but there was no diminution of his faith in his philosophy of life.

Chapter Fourteen

July 14, 1791, dawned pleasantly at Fairhill. Joseph spent a few hours in his laboratory finishing some experiments he wanted to include in the latest volume of his *Observations and Experiments*. In the afternoon he sat with his wife in their pleasant hilltop home overlooking the sprawling city of Birmingham. He was reading a pamphlet which had just been published by an Englishman, Thomas Paine, called "The Rights of Man." Joseph was enjoying it immensely. Mr. Paine attacked Edmund Burke and defended in a calm, systematic way, not only the French Revolution, but every effort to apply reason to the government of men. It was just the sort of pamphlet, Joseph said to Mary, that he would have liked to have written himself. It had been out for several months and had caused a stir in government circles already somewhat agitated by Priestley's own pamphlets.

Although he felt somewhat better physically, he was not yet quite strong. He was very disappointed that he had to give up a dinner that very evening at the Dingley Hotel with a small group of friends. They had chosen the date as the second anniversary of the fall of the Bastille in France. They were all old friends who often met for an evening of pleasant talk, and since they all felt alike about the justice of the revolution in France, it had seemed an appropriate date to get together.

Just a week before, a handbill had been distributed throughout Birmingham to the effect that some men were meeting at the Dingley Hotel to plot against the government. It was difficult for Joseph to comprehend a mind that could turn the intent of a friendly dinner into a plot against the government. The whole idea was grotesque. He had no idea who wrote the libelous paper, but he hastened to reply to it in the Birmingham *Gazette*.

"It is true," he wrote, "that a group of gentlemen is to meet at the Dingley Hotel on the fourteenth of July next. The meeting is one of many that have been held at Mr. Dadley's inn over the last several years for the sole purpose of pleasant talk among congenial friends. This meeting has only this special character, that a date has been chosen as the day on which a friendly people proclaimed their intention of no longer suffering under a despotic rule—an incident that should give joy to every lover of liberty. The charges brought by the writer of a recent handbill are too ridiculous to deserve any further elaboration."

His letter was duly published over his name and, being confined to his house and having, as usual, a great many things to do, he forgot all about it. He finished Tom Paine's pamphlet, had an early supper and sat down to a game of backgammon with his wife. It was a game he liked and played with enthusiasm, shaking the dice till they rattled like castanets. Almost all of his pieces were home, and he was shaking for what he hoped was his final throw, when his wife reached out and took his hand, quieting the rattling dice.

"Listen, Joseph," she said in a whisper.

He put the dice softly on the table and, holding his breath, listened. The door into the garden opened onto the still air of dusk. There was no wind, and what Joseph heard brought him into the garden. He stood for a moment to be sure, then hurried to the edge where he could see the fading outline of the town.

It might have been the buzzing of a bee or even the rumble of an approaching summer storm, but there were no bees, and the sky to the horizon was a pure purple. It was a human sound, and as soon as his eyes became accustomed to the dim light, he saw spots of red gold, lanterns and torches, that seemed to beat a rhythm to the rising and falling cadence of men's voices. Then into the wordless, multisyllable of sound came the crashing of glass. The sound rose to a higher pitch. Joseph knew the town well, and he knew exactly where the sounds and lights were. It was little Mr. Dadley's inn on Temple Street where, but for his illness, he would have been. His letter in answer to the anonymous writer of the scurrilous handbill had been of no avail. The fools! They actually believed that Mr. Russell, Mr. Taylor, Mr. Humphrey and all the other good men of Birmingham were schemers and plotters against the government. It seemed incredible to him, and his first thought was to get on his horse and ride to the aid of his friends.

Then his eye caught a small bright spot some distance from the Dingley Hotel. At first a blur of reddish yellow, it suddenly burst into quivering motion as a new crescendo of voices rose from around new spurts of fire. He placed this in his mind's eye, though he hesitated to believe it. It was his meetinghouse. There was no doubt about it. With the fire as a background, he could see dark figures darting about, and he could hear the sounds of hate even though the words were indistinguishable. Desecration! What had he ever done in that house but preach the truth and glorify God?

Then another sound struck his ear, nearer and easily identified—the galloping hoofs of a horse, and a voice calling his name. In the shadow of the roadway, the horse came to a sudden stop and a figure sprang off and raced across the lawn. It was his neighbor, Mr. Ryland.

"Joseph," he gasped, "they attacked Dadley's inn, broke down the door and smashed all the windows. Then they went to the New Meeting and— Look!" He pointed toward the town. A new fire had broken out. New cries arose, this time from the area of the Old Meetinghouse. "They've gone stark mad! Will they stop nowhere?"

"Who are they that you're talking about?" Joseph asked.

"I don't know—but there are hundreds of them. I was passing the inn when they were standing outside, just before the stones were thrown. I recognized only one man, the baker, John Green. He was shouting something about Church and State and long live the King, and—this is why I came up here, Joseph—he was calling your name. 'Get Joe Priestley,' he shouted, over and over again."

"But the thing's incredible," Joseph protested. "He's a Church of England man and we disagreed. That happens all the time. I took my trade away, or rather, he refused to sell me bread, but this—it doesn't make sense. Are they all drunk?"

"If they aren't now, they will be soon," Ryland answered, "Dadley has a good cellar of spirits."

The three stood incredulously watching the fires and the dancing torches. The shouting had increased and seemed to come from various parts of the town.

"You've got to leave here, Joseph." Ryland said after a moment's silence. "Green will have them so stirred up and, with the help of Dadley's spirits, they will stop at nothing. On my way I stopped at the livery stable. They're sending a horse and chaise. They'll drive you to the Russells' or anywhere you say."

"And leave my house?" Joseph remonstrated, and then, feeling Mary slip her arm through his, he nodded.

The chaise arrived. The driver reported that he was only minutes ahead of the marching mob that was obviously headed for Fairhill. He had taken a side road to avoid them, and they were not making fast time because they stopped on the outskirts of the town to break into several shops. Joseph, Mary and young Henry climbed in. Sarah was safe at Heath Forge with her husband and young Joseph was in Manchester, but where was William? He called but there was no answer. Henry ran back into the house shouting his brother's name, but still there was no answer. Was it possible, Joseph wondered, that his son had run off at the first rumor of danger? He refused to believe it. He waited as long as he dared, and then they drove off into the darkness with Mr. Ryland riding alongside. Just above the house the road went to the top of the hill and curved around and down. As they reached the crest, the sound of voices behind them grew stronger, and

137

they saw the first of the torches moving jerkily toward their house. Joseph wanted to go back to find out what or who was behind this outburst of hate, to talk to the people even if it was the last argument he would ever utter. He wanted to find his son William, to know for sure if fear had driven him to cowardice. But Mary must be taken to safety, and it was very doubtful whether he could possibly have persuaded the driver, quaking with fear, to turn back.

The Russells' house was not too far, and soon they were inside its protecting walls, comforted by Mrs. Russell and her two daughters. Mr. Russell had reached home from the hotel only a few minutes before, and he gave them an account of what had happened. Mr. Humphrey had just begun a toast to the King when a brick tore through a window onto the table. Mr. Dadley had herded all the guests downstairs and out a back door where their horses were tied. Mr. Russell had ridden home at once as had all the other men. He had no opportunity to see any of the mob, but Mr. Dadley had said that he recognized the voice of Green, the baker, a very violent and ignorant man, who seemed to be the ringleader.

Why, Joseph wondered, had John Green become his nemesis? Solid, intelligent opposition he had welcomed all his life, but the stupid, frustrating violence of ignorance was something with which he could not cope. He was discussing this with Mr. Russell when there was a loud knocking on the door and an hysterical report from a stranger that the mob was moving toward the Russell house. Whether it was because Mr. Russell had been one of the gentlemen at the Dingley Hotel or because it had

THE DISCOVERER OF OXYGEN

become known that Joseph had sought asylum there was doubtful, but doubtful or not, the frightening fact remained that terror and destruction were on their way.

Mrs. Priestley and Henry, it was decided, would be safe with Sarah at Heath Forge, and she could get in touch with Joseph Junior at Manchester. The terrified coachman was easily persuaded to drive them there, and Mrs. Russell and her daughters followed in their own chaise. There was still no sign of William. Joseph and Mr. Russell decided to stay as long as possible in order to take advantage of any chance that might arise to quiet the mob. They withdrew with their horses to a vantage point some hundred yards behind the house—and waited. In minutes it was evident that no effort on their part could have any effect. The men stormed up to the house, drunk now with their vicious successes and the contents of the Dadley and Priestley wine cellars. Cries of "Church and State!" "Down with Dissenters!" "Hang Joe Priestley!" mingled with garbled profanities aimed at nothing in particular. Joseph thought of the cries of "Crucify Him!" that had rung through the court of Pontius Pilate, and he wondered if he was going to have the quiet, humble courage of the Master, and bear his cross in uncomplaining silence. He had preached all his life—now he must practice what he preached.

There seemed to be no first blow struck at the Russell house. The crashing of glass and the rending of wood began everywhere at once, and the walls collapsed much as a sand castle crumbles under a rising tide. Someone threw a torch into the rubble, and Joseph and Mr. Russell retreated into the darkness lest the rising sheet of flame light up their hiding place.

"It's you they're after, Joseph," Mr. Russell whispered. "Ride to Worcester and get the morning coach to London. I'll go to Heath Forge with Mary and my family and join you when this is over. There's a road around to the west of Birmingham. They're not likely to be on that."

The two men solemnly shook hands in the darkness, and with a final "God bless you," Mr. Russell mounted and rode north. Joseph stood holding his horse's bridle and looking toward the red glow that marked what had been his friend's house. He knew that Mr. Russell's advice was good, and that to join Mary would only bring danger to her, but somehow running away was not in his nature. He had a strong desire to see what the mob had done to his own house. The Russell fire was gradually dying down and the human sounds were growing fainter. Leading his horse he ventured nearer. The mob was definitely going back in the direction of Birmingham. He ran over in his mind the names of his friends who had attended the fatal dinner. Most of them lived on the other side of the city, across the river Rea. This meant that the roads around Birmingham would soon be clear enough for him to ride to Worcester.

He mounted his horse and rode cautiously by the ruins. It was possible that some men might have been left on guard. But all was silent except for the sporadic crackling of dying embers, and soon even that died out into the quiet of the starlit summer night, disturbed only by the fading murmur of the mob. He rode on, soon reaching the crest of the hill where the road descended past what had been his house. He got off his horse and, leading it, moved onto his lawn. The night was bright enough to distinguish shapes and figures, and suddenly Joseph froze. A man was sitting on the ground, leaning against a part of the garden wall. For five minutes Joseph watched him, but he made no move, and as his eyes grew more accustomed to the light and details began to emerge, he realized that blood was trickling from the man's head, down the rough stone of the wall onto one of his coattails lying crazily along the ground. Joseph did not know who this man was, who moments before had been cheering for Church and State, and now was dead.

As he raised his foot to the stirrup, his eye caught sight of something on the ground. It was not a trampled flower or a broken bit of shrubbery. It was a book. He stooped and picked it up and the next moment was on his knees feverishly feeling for yards around him. There was no doubt about it. Broken bindings, torn leaves, pieces of different books had been ripped from their backs. Almost in a panic he followed their trail from the lawn for half a mile down the road. His complete library had been destroyed. Words that he had written on chemistry, politics, education and Christianity, words written by others that had inspired his own, words written with only one end in view "to find the truth of God's world" were here only a jumbled mass of matter, a paper road trampled on by a vicious mob, and leading from a dead man into the darkness. He mounted his horse and rode slowly off in the direction of Worcester.

Chapter Fifteen

Joseph knew that from Worcester he could get a coach to London, but he also knew that he would have to cover a distance of some fifty miles. Even under normal conditions this was a full day's trip, but his present situation was far from normal. In the first place he had no way of changing horses. Furthermore, the roads he would have to take were circuitous and not too well known to him, particularly in the dark. Before he had gone very far he saw two more fires break out. There were evidently roving bands of rioters abroad who might easily be attracted by the pounding of his horse's hoofs. He tried riding on the grassy shoulder of the road but there were unexpected rocks over which his horse stumbled. It was too dangerous. He must stick to the middle of the road if he were to make safe progress, however slow.

He passed Birmingham on his left, took a wrong turn at a fork and ended up in a pasture. Retracing his steps he set off again, gaining a little confidence as the stars came out more clearly in the midnight sky and he could check his direction with a certain sureness. He was afraid, not of any bodily harm that might come to him, but that he might be seized before he could reach London and report to the authorities. Surely, he thought, they will take some action against such ignorant lawlessness.

By early morning he was almost halfway to Worcester

and desperately in need of rest. He stopped at a small farm-house, knowing he was taking his life in his hands—they might have been alerted—but the farmer and his wife treated him with the common hospitality they would have accorded any tired stranger. He rested most of the day, and toward evening set out again. Reassured by the indifference of his late hosts, he crossed to the main Worcester road where he made better time. He got by the pikemen at the main Worcester turnpike gate without any trouble, and at five in the morning rode up to the Blind Horse Tavern where he knew the London coach would stop.

He was about to call for the landlord to ask what time the coach would leave for London when he heard voices from the coffeeroom, and through the half-opened door saw two early risers chatting over their ale. He pushed open the door and started across the room when he distinctly heard his name, ". . . this fellow Joe Priestley." It was what he had been expecting but it came suddenly like a blow in the dark. He had to get away; they might see him, but it was a chance he had to take. He turned, almost facing the men, but to his surprise they went right on talking about him, but hadn't yet seen him. Joseph walked on into the kitchen. There were three people, a man, a woman, and a boy, apparently preparing breakfast.

"Excuse me," Joseph said, speaking as casually as he could, "but when does the coach leave for London?"

"At eight o'clock," the man replied and, sensing a customer, came forward. "Perhaps you'd like some breakfast or a glass of ale while you wait?" he continued.

"No thank you," Joseph answered. "I'm in a hurry to get to London. Is there any post going out?"

"The post chaise leaves with the mail from the Hind and Hart at six-thirty," the man replied. "It only takes four people." He turned to the boy. "Johnny, run over to the Hart and see if you can get a seat on the post chaise for this gentleman, Mr.—er? I didn't get the name." He turned to Joseph. The conversation in the next room stopped as did Joseph's heart. "Oh, of course," he said quickly. "It's Sutcliffe—Henry Sutcliffe. I'd be much obliged." The boy ran out. The two men were talking again as Joseph passed through, keeping his eyes straight in front of him. Minutes went by as he waited outside the Blind Horse. The conversation went on. The boy ran back. Yes, there was a seat in the mail. Would the boy mind Mr. Sutcliffe's horse for a day or two? Certainly. And so it was arranged. Joseph rather outdid himself in the matter of a remuneration. He needed a friend even if he had to buy him.

Seated safely in the post chaise Joseph made a few plans. His friend Lindsay lived in Essex Street. He would go there at once. It was one place where Mary would be apt to ask for him. Then he would see the authorities and get some restitution for his losses, and punishment for the leaders of the mob. He dozed off and was dreaming that he was riding through flames on a horse to save Mary from something he didn't altogether understand, when the post chaise stopped with a jerk. It was Oxford, the driver announced, and they would start off again in an hour with fresh horses. Joseph was feeling a little groggy with sleep, but not too groggy to notice that the man opposite was staring at him. It was an uncertain but inquisitive stare, one that he felt instinctively must be avoided. The other two passengers had just left the coach, and Joseph followed them. He was in a courtyard in front of the inn door. Just as he was about to go in, a man carrying a heavy trunk came between him and the coach, and Joseph made a quick decision. Instead of going in the door of the inn, he slipped around the corner of the building and waited. He had no definite plan except that he must stay away from the man with the stare. The horses had been taken out of the empty coach, and the inn door was shut. Joseph walked quickly across the courtyard to the street, and kept on walking. If he could find another inn it was possible that he could hire a chaise, wait until the post was well on its way and then follow it to London.

His plan worked better than he had expected. He delayed until the post chaise had left, and then found a liveryman who had a single horse chaise and who, for a consideration, would drive him to London. There seemed to be no suspicion, but Joseph stayed awake all the way to London. He must be alert for any emergency.

The Lindsays received him graciously and insisted on his resting, making no plans for the immediate future. There was, of course, no word yet from Mary, but Joseph had great confidence in Mr. Russell and his own son Joseph. He worried more about William. It was incredible that he would leave his mother and father at such a time of crisis, but he *had* been in the house earlier. Joseph's first night in London was filled with confused dreams and worried hours of sleeplessness.

145

By the next day the news of the riots in Birmingham was common knowledge in London, and a few days later Mary Priestley and Henry arrived by coach. They reported that troops had restored some order in Birmingham, and an investigation was under way. They also reported something that made Joseph very happy and a little ashamed. It seemed that on the night of the riots, as Joseph was leaving the house, William hid until the chaise drove off. Then he began gathering what books and papers he could, burying them in a box in the rose garden. It had been very easy at first, but when the mob arrived, he could only gather a few at a time, and the trip from the burning house to the rose garden became more and more risky until, fearful of recognition, he left and made his way to Manchester where his brother Joseph had hidden him for a time. Mary had tried to persuade him to leave with her and Henry, but William insisted that he would go back to Birmingham when things quieted down and bring the books he had salvaged to London.

Relieved to have his family safe, Joseph turned his attention to the question of getting some satisfaction from the government, and estimating the extent of his losses. One morning he told Mr. Lindsay that he had notified Parliament that he was in London and prepared to cooperate, but had received no reply.

"And I don't believe you will, Joseph," was Mr. Lindsay's comment.

"Why not?" Joseph asked. "It's their business, isn't it?"

Lindsay was silent for a moment. He knew how trusting Joseph was, and that suspicion of evil was not in his nature.

Going to his bookshelf, he took down a thin pamphlet and thoughtfully riffled the pages through his fingers before turning to Joseph.

"Do you remember," he said finally, "writing this paper on the propagation of truth?"

Joseph nodded and Lindsay continued. "I know you often forget what you have written, Joseph, since you write so much. Let me refresh your memory by reading a paragraph to you. You wrote, 'The present silent propagation of truth may even be compared to those causes in Nature which lie dormant for a time, but which in proper circumstances act with the greatest violence. We are, as it were, laying gunpowder grain by grain under the old building of error and superstition, which a single spark may hereafter inflame, so as to produce an instantaneous explosion; in consequence of which that edifice, the creation of which has been the work of ages, may be overturned in a moment, and so effectually that the same foundation can never be built upon again.' "

Joseph looked at Lindsay questioningly. "Well," he asked, "who doesn't want the edifice of error and superstition done away with? That's what I meant then, and that's what I mean now. I don't see what harm—"

Mr. Lindsay interrupted him. "Your friends, or your so-called friends, in Parliament had a different understanding of what you meant. You don't seem to realize the seriousness of what's going on, Joseph. Do you realize that this paragraph was actually read aloud in the House of Commons? Not only that, but it was unanimously interpreted as a threat to blow up the churches of the Establishment.

147

It was even hinted that you were a second Guy Fawkes who, you may remember, concocted a little plot in 1605 to blow up the Houses of Parliament." Joseph was speechless as Lindsay went on. "You are considered to be a dangerous man, Joseph, and the leader of that thinking is your one-time friend Edmund Burke. No, Joseph, I doubt if you will get any satisfaction from the present government for what has happened. Your only recourse is to a civil suit."

It was a hard truth for Joseph to understand, and it took some time for him to accept the tragic fact. He received insulting letters. Articles appeared in *The Times* accusing him of being a traitor and an infidel. Walking in the street one day with his son Henry, he came upon a crowd burning crude effigies of himself and Tom Paine, the writer, and only quick action prevented their being recognized. Joseph remembered how on the night of the riots he had been reading Paine's pamphlet, "The Rights of Man," and he wondered if this was one of those rights. In desperation, but still with no malice, he wrote to the clergy and people of Birmingham pleading his case, but much of what he wrote was ignored or replied to in insulting terms.

He did have friends, though, and letters of sympathy poured in from such places as Bath, Bristol, Exeter and Leeds, where he had served the Mill Hill Chapel. Even from across the channel in France came letters of friendship and an offer of citizenship from the government, as well as a request from the Department de L'Orne to have him represent them in the National Convention because of his known sympathy with the revolutionary cause. This

148

last request, while well meant, only intensified the feeling against him in England. He refused the request, giving as his reason his inability to speak French fluently, and his lack of knowledge of the details of French politics. After much thought and consultation with Mary, he accepted the offer of French citizenship, considering it an honor. No sooner had his acceptance become public knowledge than he heard himself accused in the House of Commons of accepting citizenship because of his hatred of the constitution of England—and the speaker was Edmund Burke.

Any damages Joseph might hope to get would come only from a decision of the county court presided over periodically by judges of the superior courts to consider purely county affairs. His friends in Birmingham managed to secure as many as thirty-seven affidavits, not only to the actual damage done his property, but to the fact that many of the local clergy and even magistrates had encouraged the mob. These seemed to Joseph to be pretty conclusive. The witnesses were reliable citizens, the damage to his property obvious. He carefully estimated the value of his books, manuscripts and chemical equipment at what he and Mary considered a modest amount.

The court met at Warwick. Joseph Junior came over from Manchester and joined his father and William at the sessions. He himself was deeply concerned in the proceedings, not only because of his love for his father, but because of his own situation in Manchester. He had been employed in a chemical factory and had recently been married. The outlook had been bright until the riots, then his employer became worried that violence would be used against his factory because of the Dissenter's son, and he dismissed him. It was very unjust for young Joseph had much of his father's skill in chemistry, but inevitable in view of the popular feeling, and it put Joseph Junior in an impossible situation.

The affidavits were presented to the court. Legal formalities were strictly adhered to. The learned judge presided with the proper legal decorum, but the shadow of rumor and suspicion darkened the courtroom and even penetrated to the backs of the minds of the good men and true who held Joseph's case in their hands. They rendered a decision in Joseph's favor, but in an amount so trivial, so out of keeping with the loss of the product of thirty years of research and writing in theology and chemistry as to be almost insulting. There was, Joseph knew, no recourse. Hate had triumphed.

The second year in London he moved to a house of his own at Clapton, but even this move was made difficult. Landlords refused to sell to him for fear of reprisals. Even after he had finally succeeded in securing a house, servants refused to work for him, and neighbors had difficulty keeping their own servants, so great was the fear of mob violence. Joseph could easily have undergone this persecution for himself, but since it had been extended to his sons, he urged them to leave England. William went to France, planning to make his home there. He soon found the spirit of France so imbued with revolutionary violence that it became distasteful to him and, taking his father's advice, he emigrated to America. Joseph Junior had been for some time discussing with friends the possibility of a settlement in America of a colony of free thinkers. Being thoroughly disgusted with the treatment his father was receiving, he welcomed the suggestion of leaving England and, persuading Henry to join him and his wife, he sailed with his friends for the New World. It was not easy for Joseph and Mary to see their family separated, but they could not stand in their way. The boys were grown up and quite capable of taking care of themselves, and England had given them no particular cause for loyalty.

Once the affairs of his family were settled, however unsatisfactorily, Joseph set up a laboratory and with the small funds at his disposal equipped it as best he could to carry on his experiments on air. With the valuable, but limited, contents of the box that William had salvaged, he began rebuilding his library. His mind was filled with questions that needed answers. He was not yet convinced of Cavendish's analysis of water into dephlogisticated and inflammable air, and for a long time he had been toying with the idea of finding out the exact quantity of phlogiston in various metals. He hoped in this way to establish once and for all the theory of phlogiston.

Suddenly a new blow fell. It had really already fallen, only he hadn't realized it. The Royal Society was quietly, but surely, dropping him. He became conscious of it one day when he met several members in a popular coffee-house. They were sufficiently polite, but almost immediately excused themselves and left. Joseph thought back over the years of his association with this group—his first appearance before them with his carbonated water, his election in 1766, and later his work on electricity and air which won for him the Copley medal. It was hard for him to believe that true scientists would allow themselves to be influenced by the mere rumors of treason, without realizing their falseness or at least examining the evidence. Even Henry Cavendish, with whom he had repeated his experiment to determine the measurement of electric force, and who had become such a close friend, made not the slightest gesture of sympathy. This silence became a perpetual insult, and Joseph decided never again to send any of his papers to the Society. He even considered resigning until, in his practical way, he realized the value of the letters F.R.S. attached to the name of any man of science.

He missed the scientific talk of the Lunar Society in Birmingham, and now being shut off from contact with the Royal Society, he began to feel very much alone. He stuck to his belief, however, that God orders all things for the best, and very soon his faith was rewarded. The Dissenters' Chapel at Hackney, a residential suburb north of London, was in need of a minister. Dr. Price whom Joseph had met at the Whig Club years before and who had arranged his service with Lord Shelburne, had been the preacher there, and he had more than once suggested that Joseph might someday replace him. His sudden death brought the matter to a head, and the position was offered to Joseph who at first hesitated. He had always been a great admirer of Dr. Price and he modestly felt inadequate to replace him. When he found that the decision to appoint him had not been unanimous, and that one third of the congregation was afraid of possible reprisals and violence, he looked on the matter as a challenge and accepted. Here was a chance to prove that he was not as dangerous as his accusers said.

He began his preaching, and there were no unpleasant incidents. He was also asked to lecture on chemistry at the Dissenters' College at Hackney, known as New College. This was definitely an answer to his problem. Let foolish men rave about his hatred of England, let them even, as they did, liken him to Guy Fawkes or the Devil himself, he was once more in a position to speak on his two favorite subjects—theology and chemistry.

Chapter Sixteen

"Those who say—and there are many of them—that members of this institution wish to reform Church and State by violence, they are liars and the truth is not in them."

Joseph Priestley stood before his first class at New College, Hackney, in 1793 and spoke with a new strength. He used strong words because he had become bitter, and mincing matters was a thing of the past. The struggle against prejudice and hatred over the last eighteen months had worn his patience, if not his faith, rather thin. These young people were not against him. They were eager for the knowledge which he was in a position to give them, and being Dissenters they would understand his passion for liberty of thought.

He had carefully organized the results of all his experiments and observations into thirty-six lectures, simply phrased in order to be easy for the student. He remembered his own first look at natural philosophy in the pages of Gravesande in Mr. Hogue's study at Batley. Since then he had studied and verified the facts, had added vital findings of his own, and produced one hundred times more pages than there were in the Dutchman's two thick volumes. His lectures covered the properties of matter and described the different sorts of air: atmospheric, phlogisticated, dephlogisticated, inflammable, nitrous, fixed; and dealt with the fields of heat, light, magnetism and electricity.

Since his discovery of oxygen, which he chose to call dephlogisticated air, the fight over phlogiston had become world wide. Generally speaking, more people were opposed to the theory than were for it. The French, following the lead of Lavoisier, maintained there was no such substance, and they were supported by many leading scientists in England and on the Continent. Joseph had persuaded the Lunar Society of the soundness of the phlogiston theory, and even some members of the Royal Society still adhered to it.

Joseph was adamant, and in his lectures at Hackney he dwelt on it with great emphasis. He insisted that when metals or other materials were heated or burned they gave off, or lost, phlogiston, which was the substance that caused them to burn.

"The principal fact," he said to his students, "adduced by the French to prove that metals do *not* lose anything when they become calxes or ashes, but only gain something, is that mercury becomes a calx, called precipitate per se, by imbibing pure air, or what they call oxygen, and that it becomes running mercury again by parting with this oxygen. Even if this is acknowledged, it is almost the only case of any calx or residue being revived without the help of some known phlogistic substance; and in this particular case it is not absurd to suppose that the mercury, in becoming precipitate per se or calcinatus per se, as it is called in the trade, may retain all its phlogiston as well as

imbibe pure air, and therefore be revived by simply parting with that air."

Up to the time that he had passed a spark through a mixture of common air and inflammable air and found a
watery dew on the inside of the container, he had maintained that inflammable air, which the French called *hy-
drogène*, was pure phlogiston. After this experiment and
the letter from Cavendish announcing that he had found
water to consist of hydrogen and oxygen, Joseph relented
a little, and held that his inflammable air was a mixture of
phlogiston and water. He wouldn't give up the theory,
though, in spite of the growing disbelief in it, and in spite
of the fact that he himself was beginning to wonder. He
would prove it, he said to himself, by actually measuring
the amount of phlogiston contained in the various metals, a
plan he had had in mind for some time.

To do this, he first reduced the metals to their calxes
or residue by passing a spark through them. He reasoned
that by weighing the calxes before and after the process,
the difference would represent the relative amount of phlogiston in each metal. His hopes were dashed when he realized that in every case the calxes appeared to have sub-
limed or put off a gas in the process, so that he could not
be absolutely sure that he had a pure calx to start with
or even a pure metal at the end. His confidence in his pet
theory was growing weaker, but he continued to uphold
it in his lectures. He tried to weaken the position of his
opponents by attacking some of their other theories, such
as that water was made up of hydrogen and pure air or
oxygen.

"Also," he said in one of his lectures, "the union of inflammable and pure air, when they are fired together by means of an electric spark, produces, not pure water as, according to the new theory it ought to do, but nitrous acid."

He failed actually to weigh phlogiston in spite of the optimistic boast of James Watt in the Lunar Society some years before. "But," he told his friends, "neither does any of us pretend to have weighed light or the element of heat."

Joseph enjoyed his contact with the young minds at Hackney, and his congregation of the Gravel Pit Chapel, as it was called, was most friendly, but his troubles were by no means over. In 1793 the French Convention declared war on England and Holland, and England expelled the French ambassador. Anyone remotely antagonistic to the English government, or at all favorable to the revolution in France, was suspect, and many were imprisoned or executed.

Seeing all this happening, Joseph knew only too well that his position was a precarious one. Probably his contributions to science and his personal friendships with some of England's influential men would put off for a time any official action against him, but he was convinced that it was only a matter of time. His sons were getting established in America, and he and Mary were definitely coming around to the idea that they should leave England and join their children across the sea. One thing that held them was their daughter Sarah. She was happily married, and both she and her husband had no wish to leave their home, so that any such move as Joseph contemplated would be a very wide separation from his only daughter.

He had made no gesture of antagonism to the King and Parliament. He had refused the French offer of a seat in their convention. He had attended strictly to his work in the Gravel Pit Chapel and his teaching of chemistry at New College, yet he continued to receive insulting letters and to suffer the indignity of being deliberately jostled in the street. His wife had difficulties of one kind or another with servants and tradespeople, and in the spring of 1793 Joseph made it clear to his friends that he planned to leave England the next year forever.

His enemies smiled. It was obvious, they said, that the traitor was leaving for fear of being arrested, and it was urged that immediate steps be taken to imprison him. It was also said that he was not going to America at all, but to France to join the haters of England. Was he not, it was pointed out, already a citizen of France? Some of his private correspondence, salvaged from the fire by some rioters, was actually published in the papers in garbled form, entirely out of context. Joseph was reminded again of the cries of "Crucify Him," and he preached a sermon on the text, "Blessed are ye when men shall revile you and persecute you falsely for my sake." In general, however, he maintained a dignified silence.

The horror of his situation was relieved by the loyalty of his friends. A group of students at Cambridge University, where he had delivered a few lectures, sent him a handsome silver inkstand, and Joseph was very much moved and his faith strengthened when he read the inscription, ". . . from a few members of the University of Cambridge who regret that this expression of their esteem should be occasioned by the ingratitude of their country."

"I remember saying way back in the Needham days," he said to Mary, "that if I only had one member of my congregation left who wanted to hear the truth, I should be content. Here I find many, and it is very gratifying."

He made up his mind to continue his lectures up to the last minute, planning to have them published in book form before leaving England. One day he had gone down to his printer to check the copy before printing. The shop was in St. Paul's Churchyard, not far from the London Coffee House, where thirty years before he had first met Benjamin Franklin and had begun his scientific career by agreeing to write *The History of Electricity*. His decision to leave his beloved England had put him in a sort of continuously nostalgic mood, and small associations with the past seemed to assume larger proportions. He remembered how he had walked past St. Paul's the morning of his arrival, how he had stopped and gazed at the poor condemned men in Newgate Prison before going to the London Coffee House for breakfast with Matthew Turner. He instinctively retraced his steps of that long-past morning and paused across the street from the grim old prison. As he stood thinking back over the years, a rough voice, somewhat saturated with whisky, interrupted his thoughts.

"Can you see 'im, Guvner? 'E's up there orl right."

Joseph turned. He half expected some insulting remark, but evidently the speaker, fortunately, didn't recognize him.

"Whom should I see?" he asked pleasantly, not wishing to attract attention by any sign of irritation.

"Why, lor' bless yer, the bloke they're 'anging tomorrer mawning."

"Oh," Joseph replied, "I'm afraid they—er—hang some poor fellow quite often, don't they?"

"That they do, Guvner, but this fellow's been sittin' around for more'n a year, claimin as 'ow 'e did it for patriotic reasons."

The man had moved closer and was talking and breathing right into Joseph's ear. He had to be humored.

"Oh?" Joseph said, feigning curiosity, "and what did he do for patriotic reasons?"

"Started a riot, 'e did—burned up five or six 'ouses. Now yer cawn't do that, can yer, Guvner? Take me—I'm no saint, and I'm all out fer King George—but I wouldn't do nothing like that—would I? Look at me, Guvner, you and I wouldn't do—"

Joseph didn't wait to hear any more of the man's ranting. He had heard enough. Riot, burning, patriotism, King George. He remembered now that John Green's sentence had been many times appealed. Up in that dreary, iron-barred building was an insignificant man named John Green whose life had in some fateful way become entangled with his. Each in his own way had believed in God, each had considered himself loyal to his king and country, and each had felt he had a right to act as he did. Now John Green was to be put to death, and Joseph Priestley was being driven from his country. It was hard to believe, Joseph thought to himself as he turned away, that everything that happens is part of a good plan. John Green, the baker, was one of God's children as much as Joseph Priestley, the chemist, and now the life of one was ending, while that of the other was being given a fresh start. It was a hopeful thought.

The year 1793 passed, and Joseph and Mary fixed the date for their leaving England. His friends did their best to dissuade him, pointing out that at the age of sixty it was a genuine risk to undertake a sailing across the Atlantic. This was urged, not only because of the uncertainty of wind and weather, but because the Algerian pirates were preying on shipping, and he could very well end his days at hard labor, the fate, generally, of the pirates' prisoners. Nothing daunted, Joseph wrote to Lord Grenville, the British minister for foreign affairs, and requested protection against the pirates. His friends were skeptical, but a convoy was promised, perhaps, Joseph had to admit, because the government was glad to get rid of so controversial a character. As for the natural dangers of the sea, Joseph's faith in a protecting God, which Mary shared, removed all fear of them.

The date was set for March 25, 1794. Joseph arranged with Captain Smith of the three-masted vessel *Samson* to transport him and his wife for the sum of sixty guineas, bed linen not included, from London to New York. His last days were busy ones. He read and authorized the copy of his last book to be published in England, *Heads of Lectures on Natural Philosophy*. It represented to him a sort of legacy that he was leaving to the young men of England, summarizing the work in natural philosophy that had consumed so much of his time during the happy years of his sojourn in his native land. There still remained questions to be answered and natural facts to be discovered, but they would have to wait for new surroundings and the will of God.

Chapter Seventeen

For the tenth time in his life, Joseph was to change his home. Curiously enough, it seemed to him, these changes took place with odd regularity, as if Fate had decreed that he should never settle down for more than five or six years at a time. At Leeds he had promised Mary that they were in their final home, and now he was to move for the fourth time since then. He smiled at Mary and made no further promises.

Delay followed delay. Joseph preached a farewell sermon on "The Use of Christianity, Especially in Difficult Times," said good-by several times to his friends, celebrated his sixty-first birthday, and waited until wind, weather and the captain's convenience were all satisfactory at the same time. Finally, on the seventh of April, the ship *Samson*, Captain Smith in command, left Gravesend at the mouth of the river and headed for the open sea. It was a question as to whether they would sail through the channel or around Scotland, but favorable winds off Margate determined the former course, and four days later they were nearing Lands End, the last point Joseph would see of his birthland.

There were almost a hundred emigrants on board, but only six cabin passengers besides Mary and himself. They were all strangers, and lately Joseph had become a little wary of people he didn't know. He had been hurt so many times since his Birmingham experience that he had built up a sort of protective shield of caution quite contrary to his real nature.

For some unaccountable reason—Joseph refused to believe it was deliberate—the convoy of merchantmen promised by Lord Grenville did not appear, and the little ship was left to her own devices as the coast of England faded into a thin strip and disappeared altogether. The six other passengers proved to be quite friendly, whatever their political or religious views may have been, and Joseph settled down to six or eight weeks of reading, writing and conversation. The weather was rough, the *Samson* pitched and heeled in the big waves, and at one point lost two of her topsails. Mary was very sick and stayed in her bunk for three weeks, but Joseph, to his own surprise, bore up extremely well, even finding strength to help the other passengers during some of the worst days.

They passed mountains of ice and one day sighted four waterspouts, a phenomenon that was new to Joseph, although as a boy he had read about them in Gravesande's book. It was as though a column of water were formed between a low-hanging cloud and the surface of the ocean which Joseph's keen eye estimated to be twenty or twenty-five feet thick and somewhere near two or three hundred feet long. Joseph asked the captain, with whom he had become very friendly, for an explanation, but unfortunately the delay in starting and the bad weather had forced Captain Smith to find consolation in whisky and Madeira wine, and his explanation was highly confused.

He took a great fancy to "Doc" Priestley, though, and

was almost invariably at his elbow, especially when Joseph conducted a series of experiments to determine the temperature of the water at various depths. At first the captain thought "Doc" was fishing, but when he learned what he was doing he very carefully jotted down all the findings in his log with the remark, "I'll look into this later." One day he found Joseph sitting on a forward hatch reading. Glancing at the book and seeing the strange characters on the pages, he asked Joseph what it was. When he learned that "Doc" was reading a Greek version of the Bible, he was silent for a while.

"I never did get around to reading the Bible," he said finally. "In English, I mean."

Joseph smiled. He could have said, "I think you should," but he didn't. As the ship pitched and creaked, and spray slapped their faces, he spoke of God and the natural wonders of His creation. He found the captain deeply religious in the manner of most men who follow the sea and put themselves entirely at God's mercy, and there was a sincerity about his belief in God that appealed to Joseph. As a result of their talk, the captain urged "Doc" to conduct service for the cabin passengers, a duty he generally reserved for himself. Joseph agreed gladly, and extended his preaching to the emigrants in the steerage, interspersing his talks with phrases in French and German, as many of the emigrants were foreigners.

The *Samson* covered about a hundred knots a day, and on June 1 she was off Sandy Hook, and due at the Battery in New York on Wednesday, the fourth. To Joseph's surprise, a small boat hailed them before landing, and two

THE DISCOVERER OF OXYGEN

of his sons, Henry and Joseph Junior, greeted their parents and took them ashore before the other passengers. Henry was full of news for his father. He had prepared his house in Northumberland, Pennsylvania, for them to move into temporarily, and had arranged lodging in New York where they could rest. Furthermore, he laughingly told his father that rest was going to be difficult as the newspapers were already playing up his fame. The *Herald* announced, "On the *Samson* arriving this day is that celebrated Divine, republican Politician and renowned Philosopher, Dr. Joseph Priestley. No doubt that he will be hailed welcome to these climes of freedom by every friend to liberty and the Rights of Men."

This was very flattering, and Joseph modestly put it down to the usual newspaper exaggeration. But on Thursday he realized that it was much more. He was visited by Governor DeWitt Clinton, Dr. Provost, the bishop of New York, and Mr. Osgood, recent envoy to Great Britain. On Friday he received delegations from Tammany and other Democratic clubs of New York. During the first week, various civic groups waited on him, each one endeavoring to outdo the other in their words of praise and welcome. The American Philosophical Society made their words more concrete by awarding him membership in this newly formed scientific society. He received them all graciously, but in his heart what he really wanted was the peace and quiet of his own home and the opportunity for study and experiment.

He made a visit to Philadelphia, the home of his friend Benjamin Franklin, looking upon the visit as a sort of pilgrimage. There had been in his mind for some time the thought of settling there, but the bustle of the city was not to his liking. After a very brief stay, he moved to his son's house in Northumberland until he could build a house of his own. Here he would have the peace he longed for.

It was not, however, to be had so easily. A week after his arrival, the New York *Advertiser* was delivered to Northumberland by post, and Joseph read of the death under the guillotine of his friendly rival in the discovery of oxygen, Antoine Laurent Lavoisier. The accusation read that Lavoisier had poisoned the water of Paris, and added that the state "has no need of savants." As if this were not bad enough, Joseph noted that the author of the accusation was Antoine François Fourcroy, a former co-worker with Lavoisier who had been one of the guests at the Lavoisier house when he visited him with Lord Shelburne nineteen years before. He recalled the gay dinner, the light, bantering talk of pretty Mme Lavoisier, and his own stumbling description of his great discovery. What irrational thinking, what philosophical blind spot had brought hatred and death into that brilliant company of friends. Joseph was appalled.

He had always felt that Lavoisier had not been altogether fair in his treatment of him, but he had corresponded with him after the Paris visit, and as a fellow scientist he had great respect for him. It was hard to believe that France would destroy a man who had contributed so much to her scientific reputation, but then, Joseph thought, he himself had not been altogether useless to England and yet she had forced him into exile. At least, he was still alive.

On another page of the same paper, over the signature "Peter Porcupine," was a scurrilous attack on Joseph himself, reminiscent of the comments made by his enemies in England. It was quoted from a Philadelphia paper, *Porcupine Gazette*, and accused Priestley of heresy and subversion, putting a new interpretation on his visit to the United States by saying that he was an agent of the French government in America for the purpose of stirring up a revolution.

As if this were not disturbing enough, he received a very polite and diplomatic note from the secretary of Vice-President John Adams, requesting Joseph to "abstain from any political discussion lest he should get into trouble." It was evident that in the minds of many he was still suspect. From the days of Amos Woburn, Joseph had been warned to "keep out of trouble," and he had gone right ahead thinking what he pleased and using his judgment about speaking his thoughts. He would go right on doing this, but he would be particularly careful. He was in a new country which he admired. His conscience was quite clear on Peter Porcupine's ridiculous charges, and Mr. Adams' message he took as a friendly suggestion. He had his home, the beginning of a new library and his laboratory, and as time went on he acquired very firm friends in all walks of life, from President Washington and Thomas Jefferson to the humblest of his servants. Even Mr. Adams became a warm personal friend.

One man to whom he took a strong liking was Thomas Cooper, some twenty-six years his junior who, like him, had left England because of his sympathy with the French

Revolution. He was fiery and headstrong, and a most liberal thinker, which appealed to Joseph. They agreed on many things, but on Joseph's pet scientific theory of phlogiston they were quite at odds. Cooper's chemical training followed the theories of Lavoisier and the French.

"I think you're just stubborn, Joseph," Cooper said one day in Dr. Priestley's laboratory, when they had been discussing Lavoisier and his tragic end. "Lavoisier's theory of oxygen being the basis of combustion is so simple, a child should understand it."

"Simplicity isn't proof," Joseph replied. "Georg Stahl and Johann Becher were great chemists and I gladly follow them. I just don't feel that those who oppose the existence of phlogiston have made a case."

Cooper sensed an argument and followed it up eagerly. "As I understand it, Joseph," he said, "you believe that all metals are compounded of your phlogiston and a residue or calx, and that when they are heated the phlogiston goes out into the air, and when it is all gone there is nothing left but the calx. Am I right?"

"That's right," Joseph agreed, "but I would rather you wouldn't speak of it as *my* phlogiston. After all, Stahl named it a long while ago."

"Now, doesn't it make sense," Cooper went on relentlessly, "that if the metal, or whatever is burned, loses something at the end, the residue or calx must be lighter than the original metal?"

Joseph nodded a little dubiously.

"Did you weigh it to find out?"

"No," Joseph replied, "I didn't. I discontinued the experiment, because as I told my students at Hackney, I found that the calxes in every case seemed to have become partially sublimated, which meant they were not pure. I shall try again."

"You know, of course, that the French *did* weigh the metal—mercury it was—and they found that the calx was definitely heavier," Cooper said with confidence. "They claim, and I agree with them, that the calx does not lose anything, but rather gains by absorbing oxygen, or what you call dephlogisticated air."

"Or," Joseph insisted, "by losing the phlogiston which, as I explained to the Lunar Society, has the quality of levitation. Besides," he went on, "there is another substance that proves my point. I have been experimenting with what the scientists call mercuric subsulfate. It is a heavy lemon-yellow powder that decomposes into mercury but—and this is important to this argument—it cannot be revived by any amount of heat until mixed with charcoal or some substance containing phlogiston."

Cooper thought this over. "Isn't it possible," he said with a little smile, "that the charcoal merely increases the heat and thereby brings about the revived metal? Aren't you just *saying* that charcoal contains phlogiston in order to prove your point?"

"I don't believe so," Joseph said defensively. "It satisfies me. The whole phlogiston theory is certainly not without its difficulties. I realize I am in a very small minority, but I shall probably stay there till I die."

Joseph didn't feel that he was just being stubborn. He honestly believed in phlogiston. His dephlogisticated air fitted in perfectly with the theory, even if his opponents called it oxygen, and phlogiston as a substance was, to him, the basis of all chemical reactions. He decided that he would put his defense of it into writing and submit it to the American Philosophical Society for publication. Being written by a member, it would be given careful consideration and perhaps, he hoped, would convince the chemical world that he was right.

During 1795 he worked on his *Church History*, and spent hours in his laboratory. As if this were not enough work, he began preparing a course of lectures on "Evidence of Revelation," which he hoped to deliver in Philadelphia, a city he considered filled with unbelievers. He was happy because he was busy, and therefore able to ignore the libelous things that were still said of him in certain quarters.

Chapter Eighteen

The year 1795 had almost reached its end. It had been a chilly fall, and Joseph had been obliged to close his laboratory for the winter, as the frost made it impossible for him to keep his water fit for use. He was planning a new laboratory which would be properly heated, but that would take time. In lieu of conducting experiments Joseph turned to and worked side by side with Henry, his youngest son, who had a farm nearby.

The scheme for establishing a colony of freethinkers in which Henry and his brothers had been interested had been given up. The men who came from England, filled with enthusiasm for liberty of thought, found that the hard work connected with the colony was not to their liking, and they returned to England or, if financially able, settled in New York or Philadelphia. It was disappointing to William and his friends, but they realized that it would be useless to continue the scheme. William moved away from Pennsylvania, and Joseph Junior and Henry established farms of their own.

Joseph was quite proud of his ability to do hard, manual work, though he was approaching the age of sixty-three, and he spent two or three hours a day in the fields and stables. One day Henry complained of not feeling well. He developed a fever, pneumonia set in, and in spite of all that could be done, Henry Priestley died at the age of twenty. At a lonely spot on the outskirts of Northumberland, in a plot of ground belonging to the Society of Friends, Joseph Priestley conducted the final service for his son. He had been very close to him, probably closer than to either William or young Joseph, who had their own responsibilities. Furthermore, in his mind he had destined Henry for the ministry in order that he might carry on the work that had meant so much in his own life.

Mary was inconsolable, but Joseph resigned himself to the loss of his son as the will of God, and kept up his scientific and religious activities without a break. He had been cautioned by Vice-President Adams to avoid political discussion but, since nothing had been said about just listening, he sat in Congress, and listened to the debates whenever he was in Philadelphia. He told Mary that one big difference he found between English and American politicians was that while in England there were some excellent speakers, such as Burke, every one of the members of Congress in America seemed capable of speaking well.

Finding it very hard not to argue about American politics, he avoided it by concentrating his efforts on religion and science. He had come to consider the city of Philadelphia as gravely lacking in spiritual enthusiasm, and in order to strike a spark to any smoldering faith which might exist, he founded a congregation of Dissenters, stressing the Unitarian concept of Christ as a man. The trip from Northumberland was an arduous one, but Joseph made it frequently, and was rewarded by seeing the group grow in numbers and enthusiasm. Other available hours he spent finishing his *Church History* which he was beginning to feel was to be his final lifework.

He found that feeling against him in political and religious circles was gradually taking a turn for the better, although such violent men as Peter Porcupine continued their attacks from time to time. The chief point of antagonism seemed to be in the field of science. Phlogistians and antiphlogistians battled it out in letters and in the inner sanctums of scientific societies. Joseph was obviously the leader of the small group of phlogistians, and he continued his work on his pamphlet in defense of the theory. Closely allied to that of phlogiston were other theories that Joseph seemed to be almost alone in defending. Besides the composition of metals, which he constantly argued with Thomas Cooper, to him there was the composition of water. The French followed Cavendish in considering that it was made up of oxygen and hydrogen, but Joseph had often pointed out to the students at Hackney, as well as publicly, that when these two elements were combined by a spark, the result was nitrous acid and not pure water.

And so it went. Joseph felt that he was fighting a lost cause, but he had never been one to give up easily. He enjoyed battling over theories. Then, suddenly, in the midst of all this feverish activity, he suffered another bitter blow. Mary had not been too well since her Birmingham ordeal and the ocean trip, and in August, 1796, a bare nine months after the loss of her son Henry, she died. Joseph was stunned. For thirty-four years he had relied on her love and encouragement for strength to continue his battle for truth and an understanding of God's world.

174

For nights after her death he lay awake wondering if he could possibly go on with any of his old enthusiasms. Of one thing he was certain—he would never leave America now, although his devotion to his mother country was steadfast. He would stay and be buried with those he loved. He felt very much alone. Death seemed to have pursued him. As a very young child he had experienced the death of his mother and his uncle. He had the vision of the unknown man sitting grotesquely in death among the ruins of Fairhill; he heard the voice of the drunken Cockney relishing the hanging of John Green, the baker; he could almost hear the fall of the guillotine's knife as it severed the head of his one-time friend Lavoisier—and now his young son and his beloved wife.

His own health had not been too good for the past year, an attack of pleurisy had weakened him, and for some time he followed a strict diet. To avoid the feeling of loneliness, he gladly agreed when young Joseph and his wife urged him to stay in their house, which was not too far from his own laboratory and garden. With devoted friends around him, Joseph built up renewed courage to work in his laboratory. There were questions to be answered, and if Death was going to claim him soon he wanted, at least, to have tried to answer them. He had already published his *Considerations on the Doctrine of Phlogiston and the Decomposition of Water* which aroused great controversy and was promptly answered by Professor John Maclean of the New Jersey College at Princeton.

There was almost unanimous agreement among scientists that the theory of phlogiston was a false one. According to them it was oxygen that entered into materials that burned, not phlogiston that came out of them. To prove this they showed that a calx of metal increased in weight. Joseph had skilfully evaded this claim by maintaining that phlogiston had a quality of levitation. At the Lunar Society he had cited the fact that a candle flame burns up. Remove the phlogiston, he had said, and the calx naturally becomes heavier. Occasionally, shadows of doubt crossed his mind, but thirty years of defending a theory had proved his stubbornness, and his increased age did not lessen it.

There was in New York a publication known as the *Medical Repository*, edited by Dr. Samuel Mitchell, professor of Chemistry at Columbia College. Joseph turned to this as a forum for his final and rather desperate defense of his theory. He knew the opposition was international, and he had hoped to hear from some of the antiphlogistians in France, especially M. Berthollet whom he had met at the Lavoisiers. There was, however, no communication possible with France because of the war in Europe, and he turned to the *Medical Repository*.

All through 1798 and 1799 he wrote letter after letter, outlining experiments that proved his theory. To those who claimed that water consisted of inflammable air and dephlogisticated air he pointed out that when he dissolved iron and zinc in an acid solution, there was no addition of dephlogisticated air or, as they called it, oxygen, the only result being inflammable air. If water contained oxygen, where had it disappeared to?

He passed steam over red-hot charcoal and challenged his opponents to show him the oxygen which, according to them, should have come from the decomposed water. To this Dr. Mitchell promptly replied that in order to have the charcoal decompose the water, it must be exceedingly hot, much hotter than Priestley had contrived to make it. "This heat," Dr. Mitchell wrote, "must be produced by the decomposition of the fuel, of oxygen gas, or some other artificial source, and not be afforded by the water."

In dignified but persistent words, Joseph poured forth a stream of challenging questions. Why are sulfur and phosphorus formed by heating their acids in inflammable air without the slightest sign of the oxygen which, by the new theory, should be separated? Why should water be produced by the combustion of inflammable air with .77 of oxygen, and yet, with .51 of oxygen, the result is nitrous acid? What becomes of the oxygen of the decomposed water when steam is sent over red-hot zinc, and inflammable air is produced without any addition in weight to the zinc employed? Joseph was at his stubborn best, and not prepared to give up easily. He was answered, not only by Dr. Mitchell, but also by Professor MacLean and a Dr. James Woodhouse of New York. Joseph refused to be convinced and, nothing daunted, he caused a sensation in the world of science by producing a pamphlet of ninety pages entitled *The Doctrine of Phlogiston Established.* It was a repetition of the arguments he had written to the *Medical Repository* with dozens more added. It was a brazen gesture. The doctrine was not established and, in his heart, Joseph knew that it wasn't, but he said to his friend Cooper just before publishing the pamphlet, "This may be my last arrow shot in defense of phlogiston."

While the scientific world was tearing his latest pamphlet to shreds, Joseph was quietly continuing other experiments in his laboratory. It occurred to him to attempt to secure air from water by freezing. He procured a cylindrical iron vessel eight inches high and about three inches wide at the bottom, the upper opening closed with a cork and cement. In the center of this was a glass tube one fifth of an inch in diameter. In this apparatus the water in the iron vessel was frozen by means of snow and salt, the vessel being immersed in mercury, and the water contained over the mercury. When the water was thoroughly frozen by the freezing mixture, Joseph melted it by hot water. Air rose in the glass tube after each process of freezing and melting. The quantity of water was about three ounces. He repeated the experiment nine times without changing the water. He noted that the last portion of air procured in this manner was as great as any of the preceding. There remained no reasonable doubt, so he felt, but that air might be produced from the same water in this manner to an almost infinite amount. He secured two inches of air in the glass tube and found it to be thoroughly phlogisticated. He determined this by his nitrous air test, finding the air in the tube not in the least affected by the nitrous air. This experiment pleased him because it strengthened his oft-repeated opinion that water is the basis of every kind of air, and without it no air can be produced, instead of being itself a compound of hydrogen and oxygen according to the new theory put forward by Cavendish and Watt.

Sitting one evening in his laboratory by his coal fire, Joseph was intrigued by the bluish flames that flickered among the red. He had, somehow, never particularly noticed it before. Why were they blue? Was it because here was some new kind of gas being produced? He decided to find out. Since it was a coal fire, it was obvious that carbon must be one of the ingredients. He thought right away of the gas he had used to make his Seltzer water, but since this had not been inflammable, something must be added to it. His dephlogisticated air, about which there was being so much dispute, seemed to have such magic properties that he decided to use it. He carefully prepared a quantity of each gas and introduced them together into a vessel containing a glowing bit of coke. When the resultant gas was emitted, he tested it with fire, and to his delight it burned with a lambent, purplish flame similar to the one in the fireplace. When he sniffed it he could sense no odor, but it seemed to make him feel slightly ill, quite the opposite of the sensation he had when he sniffed his dephlogisticated air. This had seemed to fill him with fresh vigor. Obviously this was some new kind of gas, probably one containing very little of his dephlogisticated air or oxygen, which would account for the opposite effect on his breathing.

One day in October, 1803, Joseph had occasion to make some hydrochloric acid. He took from a shelf the bottle containing the salt he had used in his recent experiment of securing air from freezing water. He distilled the salt with vitriolic acid, diluted with an equal quantity of water. When he had secured the acid, he proceeded to dissolve copper in it, and produced good nitrous air. This result rather puzzled him, as he was quite sure that no niter had been used in the freezing mixture, nor had any been mixed with the salt. It must be, he reasoned, that the nitrogen was in the snow, and some had remained in the salt that he had retained from the experiment. This rather interested him as it seemed to prove the superstition that was commonly held by farmers around the country that snow contained nitrogen and therefore had a fertilizing effect on the ground.

Joseph was tired. He carefully noted what he had done and what seemed to be the results, closed his laboratory door and started home. It was getting dark, and his eyesight, at the age of almost seventy-one, was not the best. He stumbled over a rough place in the path, reached out wildly to grasp something, and fell. How long he lay there he had no way of knowing. His leg pained him, time and place became blurred. He came to in his bed and found his son Joseph and Dr. Benjamin Rush sitting by him. Dr. Rush, one of the signers of the Declaration of Independence and professor of medicine at the University of Pennsylvania, had for years been a close friend of the Priestleys. He and Joseph saw eye to eye on questions of personal freedom, Rush having founded the first antislavery society in America. He had attended Mary and Henry during their illnesses, and was constantly keeping an eye on Joseph's health. He found the leg injury superficial, but he was worried about Joseph's general condition. Over his protestations, Dr. Rush ordered him to stay in bed and not exert himself, and left before Joseph could think up any more arguments.

Alone with his son, Joseph's first thought was of the mysterious snow and nitrogen experiment he had just tried. Young Joseph had much of his father's enthusiasm for experimenting, and his work in the chemical factory at Manchester had led his thoughts into that branch of science. He had always followed the reports of his father's experiments and since coming to America had often helped in the laboratory. Joseph explained to him carefully what he had done, and expressed the belief that the nitrogen must have come from the snow.

"I'll try it again when I get out of this bed," he said eagerly, "but I feel sure that it proves the fertilizing power of snow."

Instead of agreeing at once, young Joseph sat quietly thinking.

"You used vitriolic acid in the distillation with the salt?" he asked finally.

"Yes," Joseph replied.

"Isn't it quite possible, then," his son went on, "that the nitrogen came from that? I've often seen you clearing black oil of vitriol with niter. Was this some vitriolic acid you had had on hand for some time?"

There was silence in the room, and for a moment no answer came from the old man in the bed. Then his head turned on the pillow and he smiled at his son.

"Joe," he said, and there was more resignation than defeat in his voice, "that's exactly what must have happened.

They say an old man's memory is the first thing to go. Perhaps it is a sign from God that I have made my last experiment."

Joseph Junior attended his father with loving care, but it was obvious that the older man was weakening. The last volume of his *Church History* was ready for publication, and the few corrections that were left he dictated to his son or to Thomas Cooper who was staying in the house to help young Joseph with the scientific parts of his father's writing.

"If I hold out till I have finished what I have on hand," he said many times, "I shall retire from this scene satisfied and thankful."

On Sunday, February 5, 1804, it snowed quite heavily. For some days the weather had been mild, and Joseph had enjoyed the fresh, sun-drenched air through his open window, but now the window was closed and he was compelled to lie bundled up in bed. He didn't like it. Up to now he had been able to sit in a chair by the window for some hours each day, although a severe swelling of his legs prevented his walking. He lay, now, and watched the snowflakes as they piled up on the window sill. Somehow he felt that the end was very near, but the thought didn't depress him. Death, he told himself, is merely a sleep before greater and more significant labors. After all, his *Church History* was finished, and his *Notes on Scripture* were well along.

Monday morning he asked Cooper and his son to take down some final notes. He watched Cooper carefully as he leaned close to the bed to catch the whispered dictation. Perhaps these were to be his last spoken words and he wanted to be sure of them. Joseph paused and asked Cooper to read back to him what he had written. He listened and a slight frown creased his forehead. He shook his head.

"That is not the way I said it," he whispered. "I want my exact words." Cooper made some necessary changes with the help of young Joseph. Then the two men waited for further dictation.

The room suddenly began to blur to Joseph. The figures of his friend Cooper and his son Joseph seemed to grow dim. I must remember them clearly, he thought to himself, and put his hand over his eyes lest the familiar faces should distort and fade. His lips moved, and the two men leaned forward. Without removing his hand, Joseph whispered, "That is all. I have done," and his hand fell from his closed eyes to the coverlet.

In 1878 a statue to Dr. Joseph Priestley was unveiled in the city of Birmingham, England. There was a crowd, but this time there was no hatred as they heard Professor Thomas Henry Huxley say, "Our purpose is to do honor to Joseph Priestley, the peerless defender of national freedom in thought and action; to Priestley, the philosophical thinker; to that Priestley who held a foremost place among the 'swift runners who hand over the lamp of life,' and transmit from one generation to another the fire kindled, in the childhood of the world, at the Promethean altar of science."

Glossary of Chemical Terms

As Used in Priestley's time	As Used in Modern Times	
Fixed air	carbon dioxide	CO_2
Nitrous air	nitric oxide	NO
Marine acid air	hydrogen chloride	HCl
Alkaline air	ammonia	NH_3
Vitriolic acid air	sulfur dioxide	SO_2
Nitrous acid vapor	nitrogen dioxide	NO_2
Inflammable air	hydrogen	H_2
Dephlogisticated air	oxygen	O_2
Phlogisticated air	nitrogen	N_2
Mercurius calcinatus per se	mercuric oxide	HgO
Minimum	red lead	Pb_3O_4

Bibliography

Aykroyd, W. R. *Three Philosophers*. London: William Heinemann, Ltd. 1935.

Caven, Robert M. *Joseph Priestley*. London: 1931.

Corning Glass Works. *Joseph Priestley*. 1938.

Dampier, Sir William Cecil. *History of Science & Its Relations with Philosophy and Religion*. London: Cambridge University Press, 1943.

Gillam, J. G. *The Crucible*. London: Robert Hale, Ltd., 1954.

Guinagh, Kevin. *Inspired Amateurs*. New York: Longmans, Green & Co., 1937.

Holt, Anne. *A Life of Joseph Priestley*. New York: Oxford University Press, 1931.

Leonard, Jonathan N. *Crusaders of Chemistry*. Garden City: Doubleday & Co., 1930.

Northumberland County Historical Society. *Dr. Joseph Priestley, the Chemist*. Sunbury, Pennsylvania: 1935.

———. *Joseph Priestley and His Contributions to Modern Life*. Sunbury, Pennsylvania: 1934.

Priestley, Joseph. *Experiments and Observations on Different Kinds of Air*. London: J. Johnson, 1774, 1777.

———. *Experiments on the Generation of Air from Water*. London: J. Johnson, 1793.

———. *History and Present State of Electricity*. London: J. Dodsley, 1767.

Royal Institution of Great Britain. *Joseph Priestley and His Place in the History of Science*. London: 1931.

Rutt, John T. *Life and Correspondence of Joseph Priestley*. London: R. Hunter, 1831, 1832.

Smith, Edgar Fahs. *Priestley in America*. Philadelphia: Blakiston Co., 1920.

Index

History of Electricity, 49, 54, 57, 67
Hogue, Mr., 14-17ff., 24, 27, 34, 39, 154
Holland, 94
House of Commons, 73, 147, 149
Humphrey, Mr., 138
Hunt, Thomas Stevy, 10
Huxley, Thomas Henry, 183
hydrochloric acid, 179
hydrogen, 127
hydrogen chloride, 11
hydrogen sulfide, 11

inflammable air, 41, 118, 125-26, 154, 157-58, 176-77
Ipswich, 31
Ireland, 112-13
Islington, 100

Jefferson, Thomas, 168
John, Earl of Sandwich, 62
Jones, Inigo, 80
Jungius, Joachim, 40

Keighley, Sarah, 14-16, 27-28
Kirkby, Mr., 27

laboratory equipment, 68, 82
Land's End, 163
lateral explosions, 51
Lavoisier, Mme., 95-96, 167
Lavoisier, Antoine, 95-98, 106-07, 118, 122, 128, 155, 167, 175
Leeds, 15, 58, 62-63, 74, 76-77, 114, 121, 148, 163
Lehigh University, 12
Letters to a Philosophical Unbeliever, 110
Leyden jar, 50, 51
Libau, Andrea, 40
lichen plant, 109
Lindsay, Mr., 144, 146-48
litmus, 109
Liverpool, 41
London, 42-43, 61, 79, 108, 125, 140, 142-43, 146-47, 150

Louis XVI, 94
Lunar Society, 117, 122, 125, 152, 155, 170, 176
Lunatic Society, 125

McGill University, 10
MacLean, Professor John, 175, 177
Macquer, Joseph, 95
Madrid, 98
Magellan, J. Hyacinth, 96, 98-100, 104-05, 110-11, 122, 128
magnetism, 50
Manchester, 137, 139, 149
Margate, 163
marine acid gas, 84
Meadows, Reverend Aylmer, 31ff., 37
measurement of electric force, 54-56
Medical Repository, 176-77
mercurius calcinatus per se, 89, 100, 155
mercury, 69, 82, 84-85, 118, 155
mice, 82-83
Mill Hill Chapel, 58, 63, 79, 148
mineral water, 40
minium, 125
mint, 83-84
Mitchell, Dr. Samuel, 176-77
Mollet, Charles W., 9
Monthly Review, 121
de Morceau, Guyan, 95
muriatic acid, 11, 69, 85

Nantwich, 33ff., 37-38, 49, 114
National Academy of Science, 10
National Chemical Society, 11
Needham Market, 31ff., 37, 49, 74, 114, 124, 159
Negroes, 131
New College, 154, 158
Newgate Prison, 43, 159
New Meeting House, 119, 125, 136
Newton, Isaac, 50
New York, 165-66, 172, 176
New York Advertiser, 167
New York Herald, 166

Priestley, Joseph, (cont'd)
establishes Sunday School class,
124; conversion of air into water,
125ff.; replies to Burke, 129; health
suffers, 130; pleads with Burke,
131; replies to handbill, 134; sees
riots break out, 136; escapes to
London, 140ff.; accepts French
citizenship, 149; teaches at New
College, 154; fights for phlogiston,
155ff.; plans to leave England, 158;
sails for America, 163; works on
Church History, 171; publishes
*Considerations on the Doctrine of
Phlogiston and the Decomposition
of Water*, 175; publishes *Doctrine
of Phlogiston Established*, 177;
tries to secure air from water by
freezing, 178; finds carbon monoxide, 179; makes last experiment,
179-82; confined to bed, 182; dies,
183
Priestley, Joseph Jr., 76, 114, 116, 137,
139, 145, 149-50, 166, 172, 173, 175,
180-83
Priestley, Mary, 57-58, 68-69, 78-80,
100, 103, 108, 114, 116, 122, 133,
135, 137-40, 144-45, 149-50, 157,
159, 161, 163-64, 173-74, 180
Priestley, Sarah, 57, 114, 130, 139, 157
Priestley, William, 70, 114, 116, 130,
137-38, 145-46, 149-50, 172-73
Princeton, 175
Prince Rupert, 116
Pringle, Sir John, 61
Pyrrmont, 40

quick lime, 105

Rea river, 116, 140
red lead, 96
respiration, 101, 103
Rights of Man, 133, 148
riots, 136ff., 146
Roman catholic, 72, 120

Royal Society of London, 56-57, 60-
62, 71, 87, 103, 105-06, 108, 110,
151-52, 155
Rush, Dr. Benjamin, 180-81
Russell, Mr., 138-40, 145
Russell, Mrs., 138-39
Ryland, Mr., 136-37

St. Paul's Church, 43, 159
St. Petersburg, 98
Samson, the, 161, 163-166
Sandy Hook, 165
Savile, Sir George, 92
Scheele, Karl Wilhelm, 89-90
Scotland, 163
Seltzer water, 58-62
Senner, David, 40
Shelburne castle, 80
Shelburne, Earl of. *See* Petty, Wil-
liam F.
Smeaton, John, 117
Smith, Captain, 161, 163-64
Smith, J. Lawrence, 10
South Seas, 77
spirits of nitre, 105, 118
Stahl, Georg Ernst, 40, 67, 169
Stamp Act, 70
Suffolk, 30-31
Sugar Act, 70
sulfur, 177
sulfur dioxide, 11
Susquehanna River, 11, 14
Sutcliffe, Henry, 144

Tammany, 166
Taylor, Mr., 37
Thales of Miletus, 50
Thorkwald, Reverend Thomas, 39
Tories, 73, 76
Torricelli, Evangelista, 22
Trinity, The, 29
Turner, Matthew, 41-44, 49, 67, 110,
159

Unitarian, 18

About the Author

WILLIAM D. CRANE was born in New York City and attended New York schools, St. Mark's and Harvard. While at college he was an editor of the *Harvard Advocate* and leader of the University Mandolin Club. A career as a doctor was regretfully abandoned as a result of being gassed during World War I. After five years of teaching English and Literature at the California Institute of Technology, Mr. Crane resigned to open his own school, The Crane Country Day School. Since his retirement in 1945, he has been a professional actor, has published children's plays, articles on education and the theatre, a book of poetry and biographies for young people.